Assuring the Future of South Sudan

Coherent Governance and Sustainable Livelihoods

Daniel W. Bromley

With contributions from

Lual A. Deng

Santino Ayuel Longar

Bishop (Emeritus) Enock Tombe Stephen

Africa World Books
Pty Ltd

A Note from the Publisher

The publisher wishes to acknowledge and thank Dr Douglas H. Johnson for his invaluable help and support for Africa World Books and its mission of preserving and promoting African cultural and literary traditions and history. Dr Johnson and fellow historians have been instrumental in ensuring that African people remain connected to their past and their identity. Africa World Books is proud to carry on this mission.

© Daniel W. Bromley, 2021

ISBN: 978-0-6450102-5-1

Table of Contents

Acknowledgement

We are grateful to the U.S. Institute of Peace for financial support in carrying out the South Sudan Institutional Readiness Assessment upon which many of these arguments are based.

Foreword

If you are a thief, quit stealing. Instead, use your hands for good hard work, and then give generously to others in need

Ephesians 4:28

The December 2013 political crisis and violence were partially resolved with the help of the Intergovernmental Authority on Development (IGAD), with important support from the African Union and the international community. Thus, we have the original Agreement on Resolution of Conflict in the Republic of South Sudan (ARCSS) signed by the warring parties in August 2015. However, the civil war resumed in July 2016. IGAD re-convened the warring parties, producing the revitalized ARCSS 2015 to become R-ARCSS 2018. This agreement was signed on 12th September 2018 in Addis Ababa, Ethiopia.

In the preamble to R-ARCSS 2018, our political leaders have committed themselves to observe the Transitional Constitution of the Republic of South Sudan, 2011 (as amended) with the following goal: "To lay a foundation for a united, peaceful and prosperous society based on justice, equality, respect for human rights and the rule of law."

These promises *must* be put into practice if we are to achieve the vision of a united, peaceful, and prosperous nation. The implementation of R-ARCSS 2018 will show whether those values have been observed after the end of the 36-month Transitional Period.

South Sudan, born on July 9, 2011 out of colonial rule of nearly 200 years since the Turkish/Egyptian invasion of the old Sudan, has not been an easy setting in which to create and sustain strong family ties and a resilient social fabric. The aftermath of several centuries of colonial devastation and exploitation was simply too overwhelming. The British/Egyptians eventually left the old Sudan in January 1956. There were also two civil wars mounted by Southern Sudanese against the central government in Khartoum—the first from 1955 to 1972, and the second from 1983 to 2005. As if those wars were not enough, the South Sudanese then fought their own civil war from December 2013 to September 2018. Those decades of war and suffering and dislocation have left a residual culture of violence among the South Sudanese. It could take generations to create a culture of peace. But it is also possible that healing and national reconciliation can come more quickly. It depends on us.

Creating a culture of peace is a long-term project—and the family is at the center of that necessary process. There will be challenges for families that have been separated by insecurity and conflict. There are millions of internally displaced persons (IDPs) and escaped refugees in neighboring countries. Families must be reunited and re-invigorated.

Sadly, there are many single-parent families struggling to get enough food. There are too many orphans and children without parental care on the street in urban settings. These are unfamiliar developments in the country we love. The traditional extended family system of our forebears has been eroded. In former times, everyone had a "home." Tragically, we now see delinquent children and criminal gangs creating threats in our towns. And worst of all, there is sexual and gender-based violence in our midst.

Despite these challenges, the human spirit of the South Sudanese people is robust. We may worship in different ways, but we understand the power of faith and honesty and good-will toward all individuals.

Human dignity and self-worth are precious gifts, and we must pledge to work tirelessly to make sure that every single person in South Sudan feels an abundance of self-worth, of dignity, of self-esteem, and of abiding hope for a better future. Each of us, in our own unique way, pray for such a future.

We share a vision and a commitment that adherence to the moral values of honesty, hard work, justice, fairness, stewardship and accountability, will guarantee that the hopes and dreams of an independent and prosperous South Sudan will never die.

Bishop (Emeritus) Enock Tombe Stephen

Preface

Lual A. Deng

The law must integrate competing interests if justice is to be done and modernizing forces are to be mobilized with minimum disruption. The strategy of transitional integration seeks to adjust the bases and therefore the roles of the traditional system without punishing those whom it benefits the most

Francis M. Deng, *Tradition and Modernization: A Challenge for Law Among The Dinka of The Sudan*. New Haven, Yale University Press, 1971, p 337].

Assuring the future of South Sudan is a product of a long conversation between Bishop Enock Tombe and my humble self about the essential pillars of a state based on a development policy forum (DPF) discourse that was facilitated by Professor Daniel Bromley in February 2014. We settled on three fundamentals of the state, which are: a) faith (moral foundation of the state); b) law (legal foundation of the state); and c) institutions (institutional foundation of the state).

Professor Bromley challenged participants at the DPF discourse in February 2014 that while South Sudan is a country (or a nation) with land and people, is not yet a state. His premise was anchored on coherent

9

governance and sustainable livelihoods as among the key requisites of a state. With relative peace, as indicated in the foreword by Bishop Tombe, I turned to Professor Bromley to undertake this Ebony Center book project. Daniel W. Bromley is Anderson-Bascom Professor (Emeritus) of Applied Economics at the University of Wisconsin-Madison. Between 2009-2014 he was Visiting Professor, Humboldt University-Berlin. Professor Bromley has published extensively on: (1) the institutional foundations of the economy; (2) legal and philosophical dimensions of property rights; (3) economics of natural resources and the environment; and (4) economic development.

The point of departure for the book is political morality – the moral foundation of the state – as one of the three pillars. Here, Professor Bromley sets the stage by focusing on the moral imperative of leadership and state, which he articulates as follows: "A moral community allows for all voices to be heard, it encourages the asking for and giving of reasons, and it creates mechanisms and processes for the peaceful resolution of the inevitable differences of opinion."

With this moral commitment—and the residual culture of conflict notwithstanding— Chapter Two of the book highlights the elements of a real economy of South Sudan beyond oil. Moral commitment ensures transparency and accountability in the use of public resources through resilient institutions for effective governance.

Chapter Three is about the legal foundation of state and Dr. Santino Ayuel Longar of the School of Law, University of Juba—and of the Ebony Center for Strategic Studies—focuses on the issue of land reform. About 83 percent of the population of South Sudan derives its livelihood from land.

The three pillars of state in turn provide the basis for coherent governance and sustainable livelihoods, which are elaborated by Professor Bromley in Chapters Four, Five, and Six respectively on agriculture, jobs, and service delivery. Professor Bromley spent a productive two weeks at New Site, Kapoeta County, Eastern Equatoria in February 2004, discussing with members of the SPLM Economic Commission, the idea of making agriculture the engine of economic growth of the South Sudanese economy. Central here is the idea to use oil revenues to fuel this engine of growth and sustainability. The time to realize this enduring idea has come, especially after the successful conclusion of more than three years of a national conversation in the form of a bottom-up grass-roots consultation of the National Dialogue process.

Chapter Seven concludes the book with the usual professional frankness of Professor Bromley. He sees serious flaws in the transitional structure of the Revitalized Government of National Unity (RTGoNU) with five vice presidents and thirty-five ministries grouped into five clusters, which he calls "confederates." Moreover, he sees such a structure not to be consistent with "transition from logic of military combat to the logic of shared governance." This chapter reminds us of the central point of transitional integration premise of Dr. Francis Mading Deng captured by the epigraph at the beginning of this preface. That is, we must use both morality and law to integrate competing interests in a "well-designed replacement" of the RTGoNU at the end of the Transitional Period. Only then will the people of South Sudan begin to reap the benefits of coherent governance and sustainable livelihoods.

CHAPTER I

The Moral Imperative of Leadership and State Creation

Daniel W. Bromley

Moral progress is not a matter of an increase of rationality—a gradual diminution of the influence of prejudice and superstition, permitting us to see our moral duty more clearly. …moral progress [is] a matter of increasing sensitivity, increasing responsiveness to the needs of a larger and larger variety of people …of being able to respond to the needs of ever more inclusive groups of people.

Richard Rorty, 1999, p. 81

I. Creating a Moral Community: The Necessary Commitment

A moral community is one that is able to acknowledge and respect the various interests and aspirations of everyone. A moral community allows for all voices to be heard, it encourages the asking for and giving of reasons, and it creates mechanisms and processes for the peaceful resolution of the inevitable differences of opinion. Most individuals have rather simple expectations of a moral community—they ask only to be respected and heard. Very few individuals expect their views to dominate the views of others. They simply wish for a voice in the on-going business of governance. Democracy is about reason giving. Imagining a moral community is easy. Creating and sustaining a moral community is a herculean task.

History teaches that the path from throwing off an oppressive regime to the attainment of a viable and sustainable moral community is exceedingly long and arduous. The 1949 revolution in China was bloody in its implementation, but it was worse in the following decades of government repression, willful starvation of millions of peasants, and the ensuing abuse and humiliation of urban elites through the Great Leap Forward and the Cultural Revolution. It took four decades for the revolutionary fever and induced terror to subside.

The Russian revolution of 1917 was equally tragic, and it too was followed by decades of totalitarian repression, the deadly famine accompanying the forced collectivization of agriculture, the Gulag, and the wholesale murder of millions of innocent citizens. Other familiar revolutions remind us that throwing off oppressive rule does not mean the immediate arrival of political and economic bliss.

It is now three decades since the emergence of Nelson Mandela from a prison cell on Robben Island and no one looking in on South Africa could possibly praise the current political and economic conditions in that tragic country. Economic deprivation continues to haunt the black population, while the political class dithers among world-class corruption and self-dealing. The African National Congress has never managed to bring about the necessary transition from a revolutionary *movement* to a coherent political *party* capable of governing. The party remains stuck in the mentality of a movement.

Its neighbor to the north threw off British rule and became independent in 1980. Now, forty years later, one repressive leader—a self-styled "president for life"—has been succeeded by another. The new president had been the chief lieutenant and enforcer of his predecessor. In southern Africa, the plaintive joke about leadership is: "Same car, different driver." Like the ANC in South Africa, the Zimbabwe African National Union-Patriotic Front (ZANU-PF) is unable—more correctly it is *unwilling*—to become a source of coherent governance. Why can't liberation movements become promising governing parties?

The answer is found in the dramatically different logics and structural attributes of a revolution as compared to governing. Revolutions and liberation struggles are top-down authoritarian endeavors. As the struggle emerges and escalates, it is gradually transformed into one militaristic regime against another. If the liberation struggle succeeds—as it did in South Africa and Zimbabwe—the victors quite easily come to acquire a sense of invincibility and righteousness. They won, didn't they? They must be worthy of governing. Unfortunately, they very often do not know how to govern.

It should be apparent that governing is a very different activity—requiring dramatically different skills, personality traits, and motivation structures—than is waging a liberation struggle or revolution. Revolutions entail *authoritarian permission structures.* "Do as I say." On the other hand, governing entails a *collaborative permission structure.* "Let us work together to accomplish shared goals." Revolutionary leaders are not accustomed to asking permission.

South Sudan won its independence in a long and tragic struggle against a regime that failed to embody the attributes of a moral community. The regime in Sudan failed the morality test embodied in the opening quote from philosopher Richard Rorty. There were long harrowing periods in which prevailing governance practices did not grant recognition and voice to those outside of the theocratic permission structure of the Khartoum government. A large share of the population was voiceless. In its oppression at the hands of the Khartoum government, it was therefore stateless.

On July 4, 1776, the American Declaration of Independence captured this simple idea:

When in the Course of human events, it becomes necessary for one people to dissolve the political bands which have connected them with another, and to assume among the powers of the earth, the separate and equal station to which the Laws of Nature and of Nature's God entitle them, a decent respect to the opinions of mankind requires that they should declare the causes which impel them to the separation.

What, exactly, were the conditions found to be lacking among those who wrote this famous document? The core idea was—and remains—that legitimate governments derive their "just powers" from the consent of the governed. When that sacred condition is violated, the people so disenfranchised retain the right to abolish those oppressive bonds. The Sudan People's Liberation Movement was animated by the same basic principle that brought the American colonies to throw off British rule. The exercise of an unjust rule violated the logic and practice of a moral community.

As we see, the unwelcome reality of liberation struggles is that too many of them replace one authoritarian regime with another. That was certainly the case in China and Russia. It would be too strong to consider the current South African and Zimbabwe regimes as oppressive on the scale of Mao's China or Stalin's Soviet Union. But it *would* be correct to insist that neither of these liberation stories has produced coherent governance that works tirelessly to bring the voices of all citizens into the shared task of sorting out goals, priorities, and honest collaboration. Corruption remains rampant, and hunger and hopelessness are the only future in sight. They are often considered to be "failed states."

II. The Essential Humility of Leadership

It is difficult for a person in a place of authoritative power to avoid supposing that what he wants is right as long as he has the power to enforce his demand. And even with the best will in the world, he is likely to be isolated from the real needs of others, and the perils of ignorance are added to those of selfishness [John Dewey and James H. Tufts, 1914, p. 226].

The transition from liberation to governance places a supreme burden of humility on leadership. As we look back on successful liberation struggles, the message is unmistakable. It is exceedingly difficult for individuals who have played a role in successful liberation struggles to undertake the necessary behavioral adjustments to become effective leaders in a new regime of governance. Effective governance is about bringing others to your side. It is about inviting them to come along, rather than ordering them to follow. It requires the ability to change places—metaphorically, if not literally.

Nelson Mandela was special because he brought moral authority to his post-prison political life. He was special not because he ordered people around. He was special because everyone wanted to come over to his side—his struggles became their struggles. Following his death, governance in South Africa reverted back to a predictable post-liberation hierarchy. Thabo Mbeki squandered all of Mandela's residual goodwill, and Jacob Zuma began his comprehensive corruption and associated pilfering of the public purse. The case in Zimbabwe has been similar—with the disadvantage of missing out on the Mandela-like brief period of hope that existed south of the Limpopo River.

The philosopher John Rawls has given us a thought experiment that could well serve as a qualifying exam for a leader in *any* government regime [Rawls, 1971]. Rawls invokes a hypothetical "Veil of Ignorance" to motivate consideration of how aspiring leaders—including all levels of government ministers and administrators—ought to think about their role. The Veil of Ignorance asks each individual to consider what sort of governance structure and procedures they would advocate without knowing what role they would occupy once the Veil is lifted and they were required to assume a randomly assigned role. Think of this as being in a room where you must vote for but one of a variety of structures and governance procedures that could be adopted. Then, after voting, you leave the room and are handed a slip of paper revealing that you must now assume the life—the lived experience—indicated on that slip of paper. Are you assigned a life as a high government official or as a truck driver?

Rawls suggested that the most likely "constitution" adopted under this form of a "blind taste test" would be one that afforded the greatest scope for individual freedom and equality regardless of the individual's ultimate role in society. Whether assigned a life as cattle herder, shop clerk, village leader, teacher, or government minister, each individual would be most likely to have voted for a "constitution" that offered the greatest probability of a meaningful and prosperous life. We might think of this as a "no regret" constitution. Once individuals had voted, left the room, and assumed the role assigned to them on that slip of paper, they would not wish to trade places with any other individual in society. That condition would signal a *just* constitution, and the promise of a viable moral community.

Imagine an aspiring politician or government leader facing the prospect of an assigned life ruled by the actions of others. That alone would serve, in the Rawls experiment, to induce ministers and government employees to support a constitution that would assure equitable treatment of everyone. And it would cause them to favor behavioral rules and expectations on them that—were they to occupy a different role in society—would leave them reassured that governance was honest and effective.

Upon reflection, the Rawlsian Veil of Ignorance is simply the constitutional variant of the Golden Rule. Govern as you wish others would govern if they were given the chance. It is also the "Categorial Imperative" of the German philosopher Immanuel Kant: act (govern) as if your behaviors were codified in a set of rules that all individuals would willingly abide by.

III. The Urgent Steps of Leadership: Institutional Innovation

The Rawlsian Veil of Ignorance reminds us that the truly moral community is one in which all individuals have a stake—a vested interest—in both the means and the ends of governing. Aristotle insisted that all citizens must be regarded as partners in the on-going task of governance. In this way, everyone will wish to have both honest government, and equitable outcomes. Aristotle saw coherent governance as a partnership, and he insisted that all citizens must be educated and committed to preserve that partnership. Aristotle was interested in what we might call "reciprocal equality." And this brings us back to Rawls. The essence of the Rawlsian Veil is to bring about a commitment to a "constitution" and a pattern of governance that is acceptable to all—regardless of their station in life. The formal institutions and practices of a regime are important—as will be seen below. But the moral character of the citizens is also important. It is not just leaders who must make a commitment to a moral community. Every individual citizen must make an equal commitment.

We are concerned here with the moral imperative of state creation. South Sudan became an independent *nation* on July 9, 2011. Now, nine years later, it is still not a coherent *state*. A nation is not a state. Nations are officially recognized autonomous entities, given official sanction by membership in the United Nations. Nothing in the international recognition of nationhood implies that such entities qualify as states. Indeed, a large number of websites are devoted to documenting just how defective many of those nations are (Transparency International, Freedom House, etc.).

Some nations are defective because they have not yet managed to create plausible governance structures and protocols that enable them to carry out the *people's business*—they are "failed states." This raises the question about what is the difference between a nation and a state?

As above, a nation is an internationally acknowledged geographic domain over which a government presides. A nation occupies a piece of Cartesian space on the surface of the earth, that is then conveyable to a graphical representation of that occupied space—a map. But this empirical reality tells us nothing about whether or not that empirical reality is a coherent, functional, operational, and accountable political community. Few would regard North Korea as an accountable state. It is a dictatorship. A state is a viable moral community offering its citizens voice, security, opportunity, and autonomy. North Korea fails on these conditions. A state is, therefore, much more than an empirical trace on a map. It is a governing going concern. A state is not the mere presence of a government. That is necessary but not sufficient.

If a nation is to qualify as a moral community it must offer its residents (citizens) a measure of Aristotelean "partnership." This can only be achieved by the creation of two essential components. First there must be a comprehensive legal structure—a governing architecture—that creates clear behavioral norms for all individuals, including government agents. Second, there must be equally transparent procedural rules so that the processes of governance are clear, standardized, and open to revision. We see that the first condition is structural in nature, while the second is procedural. These necessary structural and procedural parameters are *institutions*.

A. The Necessary Structural Parameters

It is sometimes thought that institutions are organizations—a ministry, a university, a government department. This is mistaken. Institutions are the *working rules* of a nation. Institutions specify what individuals *must* and *must not* do, what they *may* do without interference from other individuals, what they *can* do with the aid of collective authority, and what they *cannot* expect the collective authority to do in their behalf [Bromley, 1989, 2006].

The functions and programs of governmental organizations are defined by the institutions (the rules) that created those organizations. The Ministry of Finance carries out its specific roles and obligations

THE MORAL IMPERATIVE OF LEADERSHIP AND STATE CREATION

What are Institutions?

Institutions are collectively determined rules by which people sharing common citizenship of a nation-state agree to carry on their daily life. Customs and traditions are the informal variant of institutions. The formal variant of institutions are the legal parameters that indicate boundaries of acceptable individual and social behavior. Institutions demarcate authorized transactions in the market. Institutions are the "working rules" of a society.

in accordance with the legislation that created that Ministry. We see that institutions are the "blueprints" for organizations. If governmental organizations do not function well, the reasons for that failure can often be traced to the institutions (the blueprints) that created those organizations. Perhaps the organization was incorrectly designed. Perhaps personnel policies—a specific class of institutions—are flawed.

Institutions empower actions by specifying permissible behaviors. The Ministry of Finance may issue policies (rules) concerning interest rates, but it may not issue policies (rules) concerning labor practices. Institutions define authorized versus prohibited behaviors. Institutions specify how employees must be treated, whether industrial wastes can be discharged into rivers, and the tax rate on earned income. Institutions define what is possible, and what is impermissible. A well-functioning society—and economy—is a *constructed order* whose central purpose is to minimize and mediate conflict arising from scarcity. This constellation of rules—institutions—comprises the parameters of how an economy will function.

The quality of a nation's institutions—like the quality of an automobile engine—determines how well the state will perform these necessary functions. A focus on institutional quality concerns whether or not the structural parameters—the legal and customary working rules—of a nation give rise to behaviors that, in the aggregate, deliver sustainable livelihoods and a sense of collective well-being.

The above definition calls attention to the **collective authority**. The collective authority is a nation's government—the legislative

21

component, the executive component, and the judicial component. These three components are created and sustained for the purpose of defining acceptable behaviors in society. This determination of acceptable behavior is constantly undergoing adjustment through new public policies. The dynamic aspect of institutions concerns these ongoing processes of adjustment in response to new scarcities, new information, new relative values, and new ideas concerning shared social goals.

Because governance is an Aristotelean partnership, the essential characteristic of a plausible moral community—a *state*—is the opportunity for contested reason giving. Citizens must be able to participate in the on-going business of governance. Honest governance is necessarily an on-going dialogue involving those who govern, and those who are governed. Periodic elections are opportunities for a *collective conversation* about desired directions in the future. However, elections are not about voting. Elections are about reason giving. The reasons concern which new institutional arrangements (policies) now seem better than the *status quo* institutional structure.

Institutions are constantly in need of adjustment, updating, and refinement. This continual need for monitoring, assessment, and inevitable adjustment is the essence of *governance*. So we see that coherent governance entails structures, as well as a means to modify those structural attributes.

B. The Necessary Processes

The business of governance entails constant attention to emerging problems—floods in the far west, crop failure in the north, drought in the east, labor problems in the capital city, and washed out roads somewhere else. Governing is a non-stop exercise in managing the unexpected, anticipating the probable, and preparing for the unknown.

These necessary adjustments and adaptations—generally referred to as new policies—entail the necessary adjustments in the institutional architecture of a nation. This need for change arises in response to new conditions and imperatives. Political communities—states—that cannot bend will break. Policy reform is preferred to revolution. The process of reform concerns public policy. Policy reform is the active component of governance.

Coherent governance requires being alert to defective social outcomes—especially livelihoods—and launching new public policies to rectify observed flaws. The economy is always, and necessarily, in the process of becoming.

IV. Sustaining Coherent Governance

Governance is a necessary process of continually adjusting the specific nature and content of a nation's institutions. This is a negotiated process in which different individuals and groups of individuals seek to have their specific interests protected by the granting of preferential treatment. This preferential treatment entails the granting of a *right* by the political community (the state) through its government. Rights enable and empower specific behaviors. Against this newly established right will stand others who now bear a new *duty*. Duties prohibit specific behaviors. This inevitable contestation over rights and duties—redefining domains of acceptable behavior—is the essence of public policy. Because this process is always contested, we may think of public policy—institutional change—as a process of *institutional transactions.*

The three essential compo-nents of public policy are: (1) the behaviors of members of a society; (2) the institutions that define the acceptable scope of these behaviors; and (3) the prevailing beliefs that underpin

> **Institutional Transactions**
>
> Public policy is an activity carried on by legislators, judges, and administrators as they modify the legal foundations of the state. Since these changes are always contested, negotiated, and worked out with the attention of various interests in a society, it is correct to consider public policy as an example of institutional transactions.

23

(justify) that specific institutional structure. This institutional structure is best understood as a reflection of prior beliefs about desired behaviors.

However, today's institutions—mirrors from the past—often fail to bring about acceptable behaviors when conditions change. When citizens seek legislative or judicial relief from new unwanted outcomes, they are motivated by the hope of bringing about new institutional arrangements—new laws—that will correct those flawed outcomes. If agricultural credit is not available, or too expensive, agricultural interests will seek to remedy that flawed outcome. If transportation options are defective, new institutions will be sought to correct that defect.

Emerging concerns with existing behaviors and outcomes cast doubt on the efficacy and suitability of prevailing institutions that are the reasons for those defective behaviors. Gradually, shared beliefs about the suitability of those institutions (and their implied behaviors) induce institutional change. In the absence of desired institutional change, these unwanted behaviors and their outcomes persist. If dissatisfaction is severe and widespread, there may arise threats to civic peace. Redesigning institutions can meliorate social discord.

Notice the causal sequence here—beliefs about proper behaviors explain the existing institutional arrangements, which in turn influence and reinforce (explain) the associated behaviors, which then produce a constellation of social and economic outcomes. That is: beliefs → institutions → individual behaviors → particular social and economic outcomes.

Individual behaviors consist of the daily patterns of actions and interactions among citizens. Herding patterns, specific farming systems, conditions and hours of work in commercial firms, and rates of pay for various occupations are examples of behaviors in an economy. When aggregated, these individual behaviors constitute the performance of an economy.

As above, institutions define and specify accepted and prohibited action for individuals. *A coherent economy is predicated on an ordered constellation of working rules.* This order gives rise to agreeable performance of an economy. Many developing countries are accused of harbouring corruption. However, the central problem in poor economic performance is very often *not* corruption. Rather, inadequate or missing institutions lead to perverse individual behaviors, thereby undermining economic performance.

The performance of an economy is determined by the beliefs that individuals hold about that economy—and how it performs. It is from this constellation of perceptions that individual are able to create their best economic strategy for survival—should they invest in new machines for their business, should they look for a different job, etc.? Beliefs comprise perceptions and understandings of our everyday existence. Beliefs are of two kinds (1) *framing*; or (2) *instrumental*. *Framing beliefs* reveal how we imagine the world to be. *Instrumental beliefs* reveal a presumed causal structure that informs how we will interact with that framed world. Framing beliefs are structural, while instrumental beliefs are behavioral.

It is here that the realm of beliefs brings pressure to bear on the realm of rules—institutions. The necessary animation is some new pressure against the prevailing pattern of settled beliefs concerning what is considered good. When expectations are undermined, collective dissatisfaction threatens social peace. This process of institutional change is shown in Figure 1.1.

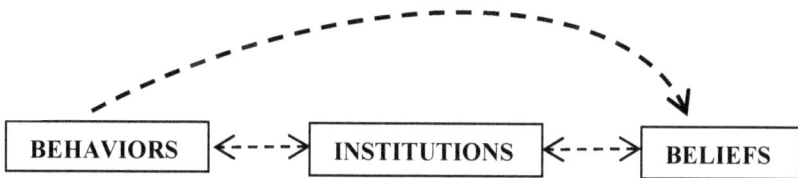

Figure 1.1 Public Policy as Institutional Change

A coherent state is always "cycling through" the three realms. New beliefs—animated by the emergence of unwanted outcomes arising from specific behaviors—give rise to a quest for modified beliefs about the ideal structure of institutions. Once there is emergence of new beliefs about particular behaviors, the policy process begins. Eventually a new institutional innovation will emerge to redefine acceptable behaviors. The economy becomes by a continual process of re-creating the institutional arrangements that redefine accepted individual behaviors.

New beliefs inform and rationalize new institutions that lead to changes in behaviors. Those new behaviors produce outcomes that will be judged good or bad, and those assessments will then signal to the realm of beliefs that things are now fixed—or that yet further institutional manipulation is called for. Governance is a process of institutional adjustment.

V. Implications

The much-prized Aristotelean partnership called good governance, like national independence itself, must be fought for and vigorously defended. Coherent governance involves a sacred partnership in which those who govern are held accountable to those who are governed. When that partnership is sustained we can say that a nation has become a state. Until that time, a nation remains a mere playground for politicians.

South Sudan now rests at the most precarious point in its brief history. Voting for independence from Sudan was easy. The joyful parades and celebrations on July 9, 2011 were cathartic. But the bliss of independence and political autonomy has now long dissipated. What remains is petty political disputes, refugees and internally displaced persons, aggressive hunger, unemployment, and predatory youth gangs.

There is also no one else to blame. President Omar al-Bashir is no longer available for hatred. Islam is no longer the enemy. Who is left to blame?

REFERENCES

Bromley, Daniel W. 1989. *Economic Interests and Institutions: The Conceptual Foundations of Public Policy*, Oxford: Blackwell.

Bromley, Daniel W. 2006. *Sufficient Reason: Volitional Pragmatism and the Meaning of Economic Institutions*, Princeton: Princeton University Press.

Dewey, John and James H. Tufts. 1914. *Ethics*, New York: Henry Holt.

Rawls, John. 1971. *A Theory of Justice,* Cambridge: Harvard University Press.

Rorty, Richard. 1999. *Philosophy and Social Hope*, New York: Penguin Books.

CHAPTER 2

Beyond Oil: The Urgency of a Real Economy

Daniel W. Bromley and Lual A. Deng

I. The Perils of Oil Dependence

The presence of oil in South Sudan is not a blessing but a curse. Oil has distorted the minimal post-war economy and turned the country into a passive supplicant of the international oil market. As a result, national independence in 2011, so long pursued and so tragically acquired, has brought continued dependence and persistent economic dysfunction. Despair is widespread. This is not what independence was supposed to bring.

Meaningful nation-building is impossible unless the people of South Sudan can take control of their own precarious economic future. Doing so requires defeating the curse of oil. In addition, sustainable peace requires liberation from a new enemy—foreign opportunists who rely on South Sudan's oil exports. A former domestic enemy during the long civil war has now been replaced by a collection of foreign adversaries

The Curse of Oil

There are many reasons why oil is dangerous for weak states. Norway can deal with the many threats because Norway is a well-disciplined state. Few African nations can manage the threat. Angola, Gabon, Equatorial Guinea, and Nigeria demonstrate the political and economic harms that can arise from oil.

Oil revenues are dangerous because they flow directly into a nation's treasury rather than as export income earned by independent (private sector) firms who hire workers, purchase necessary productive inputs, pay taxes, and generate business for affiliated companies (the multiplier effect). The geographic concentration of oil production in South Sudan means that oil is its own small isolated enclave economy with minimal connection to the rest of South Sudan.

who care little about the lives of South Sudanese. The country needs international partners to help it achieve sustained growth and development. Foreign oil buyers do nothing in that regard.

The curse of oil corrodes and undermines the development of a viable private sector that is necessary to deliver meaningful employment and plausible livelihoods for present and future generations. Entrepreneurial decay and corruption are the inevitable result of an oil economy.

The peril of reliance on oil is seen in the price history of this volatile export commodity. In Figure 2.1 we show the real price of oil since 1965, marking the events that induced profound price shocks. We see that South Sudan gained its independence just as the price of oil was rising. The outlook was auspicious. But of course 2014 brought harsh reality. Suddenly, the source of most export earnings lost its luster. More recently, Saudi-Russian machinations over oil have introduced new price uncertainty into an already-uncertain commodity. In the core-periphery model introduced by Raul Prebisch, South Sudan is at the outer periphery of the world economy and is a helpless price-taker for its only feasible export [Prebisch, 1962]. South Sudan is dangerously dependent on a fickle market for a commodity that is on the wrong side of energy history.

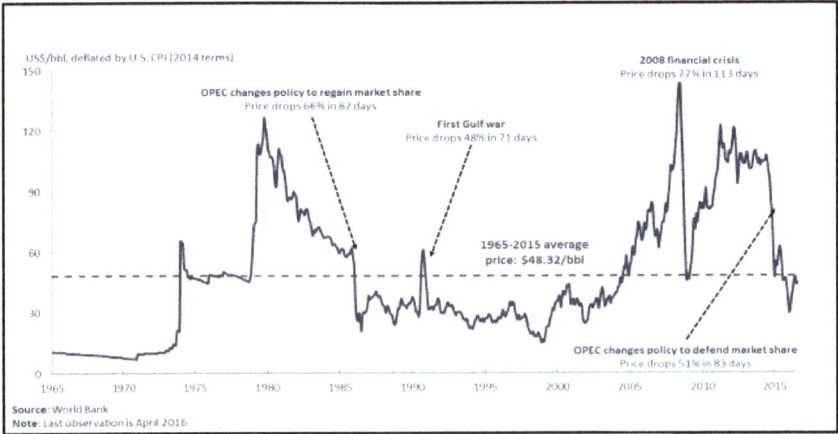

Figure 2.1. Real World Oil Prices since 1965

In fact, Figure 2.2 reveals the precarious economic circumstances for countries that are dependent on the export of all natural resource commodities. Recall that most African countries gained their independence during a period of favorable commodity prices. Unfortunately, from the mid-1970s onward, it has been a perilous trajectory. The optimistic interregnum that began around 2000 did not last. As above, South Sudan, a newly independent country in the middle of 2011, has been victimized by bad timing. That was the year global commodity prices crashed.

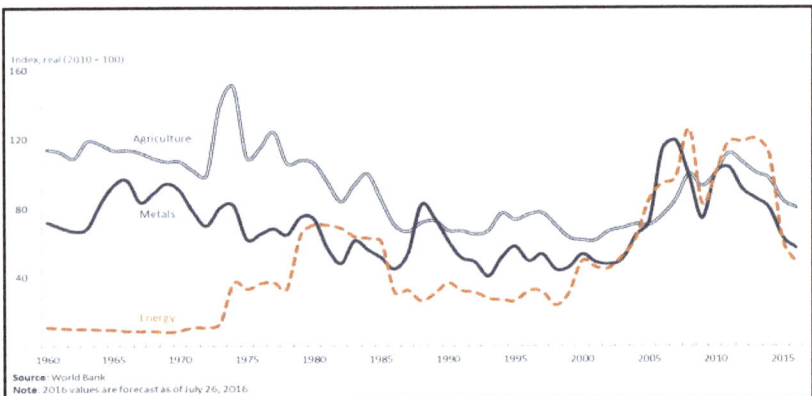

Figure 2.2. Index of Real Prices of Three Classes of Primary Commodities

30

To see the extent of the crash, consider Figure 2.3. This covers the period beginning in 2011. The only commodity showing an increase between 2011 and 2014 was oil. But, the Government of the Republic of South Sudan (GRSS) shut down, voluntarily, its own production in January 2012. It resumed production in April 2013, but in 2014 the world price of oil collapsed. South Sudan could not have picked a worse time to have shut down its oil production over transit fees with Sudan. Everyone was betting on oil. It turned out to be a bad bet.

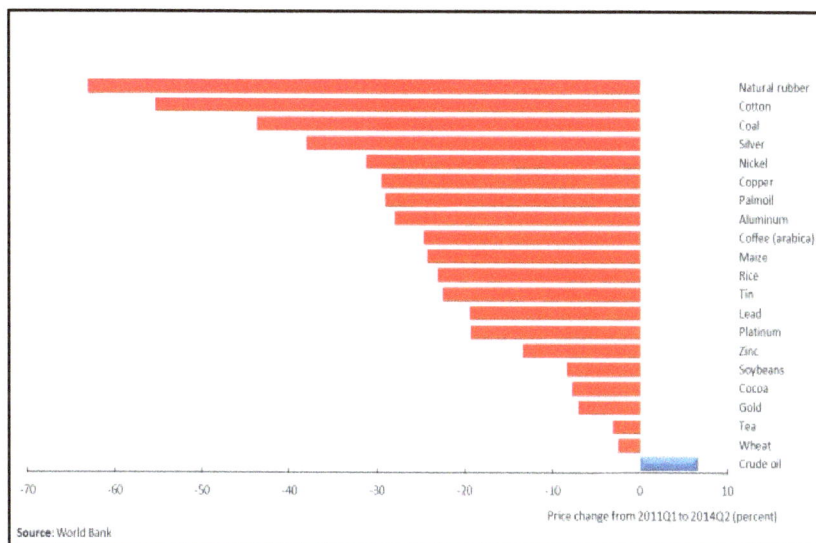

Figure 2.3. Percent Change in Real Commodity Prices 2011-2014.

These three figures reveal just how dangerous it is for a small developing country to survive—and to thrive—as an exporter of primary commodities. Escape from the curse of oil requires a multi-year commitment to create and sustain development strategies that give rise to a real (non-oil) economy that can: (1) remain free of corruption; (2) respond to economic incentives; (3) contribute to economic coherence; and (4) be receptive to international advice by honest development partners. A robust private sector is the *sine qua non* of a promising political and economic future for

South Sudan. The nature and extent of current economic dysfunction in South Sudan is illustrated in Table 2.1.

	South Sudan	Rest of Sub-Saharan Africa *(42 countries)*
Borrowers from Commercial Banks (per 1,000 adults)	1.2	65.0
Foreign Direct Investment (% of GDP)	–0.1	4.7
General Final Consumption (% of GDP)	65.5	15.3
Gross Capital Formation (% of GDP)	4.2	24.3
Gross Fixed Capital Formation (% of GDP)	4.1	23.3
Inflation (consumer prices annual rate)	206.8	6.8
Industrial Value Added (% of GDP)	21.2	24.4
Manufacturing Value Added (% of GDP)	4.3	10.6
Services Value Added (% of GDP)	67.1	45.6

Source: World Development Indicators

Table 2.1. The Missing Real Economy (average of 2015-2017)

Here we see that in comparison with 42 other countries in sub-Saharan Africa, just over one adult in 1,000 has been served by a commercial bank (compared to 65 adults in the rest of the Continent). Foreign direct investment as a percent of GDP is non-existent, the government is the main consumer of final consumption (because there is little private consumption), capital formation as a share of GDP is anemic, inflation is severe, manufacturing as a share of GDP is very low, and the service sector as a share of GDP is very high.

This latter figure is not a sign of an advanced and modern South Sudanese economy in which the service sector dominates. Rather it signals quite the opposite. This large share of services in GDP is explained by the fact that South Sudan is the world's major recipient of international humanitarian assistance, and the service sector thrives on the dominance of ex-patriot advisors and visitors in Juba (and elsewhere throughout the country). Moreover, services comprise a large share of the total economy because of the absence of manufacturing, and the debilitated state of agriculture. All of these factors are signs of profound economic duress and weakness.

In addition to the above difficulties, the macroeconomic dangers of oil states are well known. Exchange rates become distorted, domestic wage structures are mis-aligned, and other productive activities are placed at a comparative disadvantage. What is less obvious—but of greater importance in developing countries—are the "two c's" of oil-dependence: (1) *capital* intensity; and (2) geographic *concentration*.

The basic problem with oil states that lack a real economy, and are therefore flooded with unemployed labor, is that oil production and transport are extremely capital intensive. The ratio of capital assets to total revenue is higher in oil production than in most other industries. In labor-surplus economies such as South Sudan, the extraction and transport of oil is the essence of an **enclave economy**. That is, the oil economy functions in rather complete isolation from the general economy. In its isolation, it fails to be a source of employment and hope for most citizens.

On the matter of geographic concentration, the oil fields of South Sudan are highly compact and they straddle the new border with Sudan. In consequence, much of the country's oil production occurs very close to the northern border, thus contributing to the potential for armed conflict. This remote location of oil production, coupled with the absence of employment opportunities, means that the oil sector is economically irrelevant to the vast majority of the population on either side of the shared border.

The perils of oil dependence are magnified and reinforced when a country is also emerging from years of civil war and the ravages that entails. South Sudan is twice vulnerable.

II. The Perils of a Post-Conflict Country

Although the particular effects of conflict depend on the characteristics embedded in the root causes of civil wars, as well as on the specifics of the conflict (intensity, duration, territorial location and so forth), there are common effects of conflict that can be summarized in broad terms as "stylized" facts of a post-conflict transition. A review of post-conflict literature tends to indicate that violent conflict more often than not creates a series of impediments to the creation of a viable economy [Mack, 2002; Bromley and Anderson, 2012]. The durable burdens are several.

A. Destruction of Physical Infrastructure

During extended conflict, a broad range of economic activity necessarily contracts into self-sufficient enclaves of subsistence production and consumption. This contraction is necessitated by the inability to move economic inputs and products across space. It is normal in such circumstances to regard the problem as one of degraded physical infrastructure—roads, bridges, and the scarcity of trucks, trailers, and necessary fuel. But this undesirable autarky also reflects a breakdown in the security of economic activity across space. It is impossible for markets to work if the movement of goods is imperiled by theft and destruction. A related loss comes in the public provision of services—education, health facilities, water and sanitation, and communications systems.

A viable post-conflict economy is jeopardized by general degradation or destruction of most essential infrastructure. The urgent need is the rehabilitation of transport systems (e.g. road networks), telecommunications, public utilities (e.g. electricity and water), etc. Rehabilitation of these systems sends important signals to the private sector that it is now prudent to participate in the post-conflict economic recovery and reconstruction. Doing so would provide an immediate boost in necessary employment and growth at the early stages of the war-to-peace transition.

B. Loss of Human Capital

A second lasting residue of civil conflict is that the very best human resources have been engaged in war, or they have escaped the country for safety and economic security elsewhere. This exodus is related to a general breakdown in civil peace so that no one feels safe engaging in commercial activities. When peace finally arrives, it can take considerable time before non-combatants feel comfortable venturing far afield from their home base. As above, economic activity shrinks into small local spaces in response to the diminished conditions of law and order.

The central challenge is thus to re-build an inclusive, efficient, and effective civil service system, as well as the legal arrangements—the institutions—necessary for a functioning market economy [Bromley, 1989, 2006, 2008; Easterly, 2001].

C. Degraded Public Financial Management Systems

On the government side of the economy, civil conflict often destroys systems of accountability and transparency in the management, mobilization, allocation, and utilization of public financial resources. Often, corruption and misuse of public funds is the unwelcome result. New public financial management systems are required to ensure that the budget is a "financial mirror of society's economic and social choices" [Schiavo-Campo and Tommasi, 1999].

D. Destroyed Civic Engagement

The most serious problem is the loss of trust and "social capital" within a country recovering from civil conflict. There is a heightened need for enhanced social stability, community cohesion, and healing in the aftermath of conflict [Easterly, 2001]. Robert Putnam uses the term *social capital* to describe the "… reserves of mutual assistance created through norms and networks of civic engagement, just as monetary capital accumulated through one set of activities to others, thereby mobilizing collaborative action to further community well-being [Putnam, 1995, p. 256]."

Trust, the essential ingredient in a well-functioning market economy, disappears in an environment of a violent conflict and trust must be reestablished as one of the essential enabling conditions. Until trust and the necessary legal architecture—institutions—can be recreated, the shipment of products is inhibited in a legal vacuum in which the security of ownership of cargo is uncertain. The financial arrangements for movement of goods across space are difficult to arrange in the context of generalized mistrust. Trust is essential.

III. The Path to Progress[1]

Several "stylized facts" guide economic thinking about creating a real economy in post-conflict countries—an economy that transcends the addiction to oil. These are: (1) the positive correlation between savings rate and the level of per capita income [Steger, 2001]; (2) institutions and governance are key sources of difference in economic performance across countries [Bromley, 1989; Bromley and Anderson, 2012; Easterly and Levine, 2001]; (3) the capital/output ratio is roughly constant over long periods of time [Kaldor, 1961]; (4) the rate of return on investment is roughly constant over long periods of time [Kaldor, 1961]; and (5) economic activity tends toward concentration [Easterly and Levine, 2001].

Running through each of these stylized facts is the inevitable and crucial nexus of labor and capital. If countries can get that essential nexus to function well, then this means that long-run commitments between owners of labor and capital will emerge, household incomes will begin to rise, the new income will begin to be spent, this will generate gains from employment and income multipliers, and gradually "economic growth" will begin to occur. But it will occur not because the government decided growth was good. It will occur because the government—and the various donors—put in place a set of policies

---

1   This and the following section are based on Lual Deng, et al., 2012.

(institutional arrangements) to make sure that labor and capital could become engaged over the long term.

It is necessary to recall that economic growth and poverty reduction are the end results of a very long process that starts with employment. Stated differently, economic growth is not something that countries (or governments) "do." Nor is poverty reduction (or eradication) something governments "do." What governments "do" is to create, through appropriate policies and coherent institutions, the settings and circumstances in which labor and capital can come together to the benefit of owners of capital, and those who own only their labor power. These two forces of constructive change come together in labor markets. This is the capital-labor nexus. Labor cannot perform in the absence of a direct connection with capital, and capital is worthless in the absence of a connection to labor. That is why Marx called capital the "means of labor." It is essential to pay great attention to that essential nexus.

If economic growth can be achieved, it is still no assurance that a large share of the population in South Sudan can rise above the poverty line of less than $1.25 a day. Addressing this problem will require a suite of policies (institutional arrangements) adopted by the government. The important point, however, is that the majority of South Sudanese people would be working and earning money. With this situation stabilized, they could then start spending. This gradual infusion of liquidity into the countryside would begin to produce important multiplier effects. Gradually the economy of South Sudan would start to work as it must if poverty is to be reduced and eventually eradicated.

Economic development is about improvements in living standards supported by productivity growth. Development also requires a constellation of social change associated with urbanization, the emergence of a larger middle class, and the drive toward greater gender equality. All these transformations are related to an economy's ability to create jobs. The development process is about some jobs becoming better and others disappearing, about some people taking jobs and changing jobs, and about some jobs migrating to other places, within and across countries.

Development as structural change often entails the movement of labor from rural, agricultural, and mostly subsistence activities to urban, non-agricultural, and mostly market-oriented activities. This movement involves transformations in the lives of families, adjustments in the organization of firms, and gradual evolution in the norms and values—and habituated behavior—of members of societies. This process can boost productivity and improve living standards, but it also affects the cohesiveness of society. Jobs can thus be seen as the "hinge" connecting three transformations at the center of economic development (Figure 2.4).

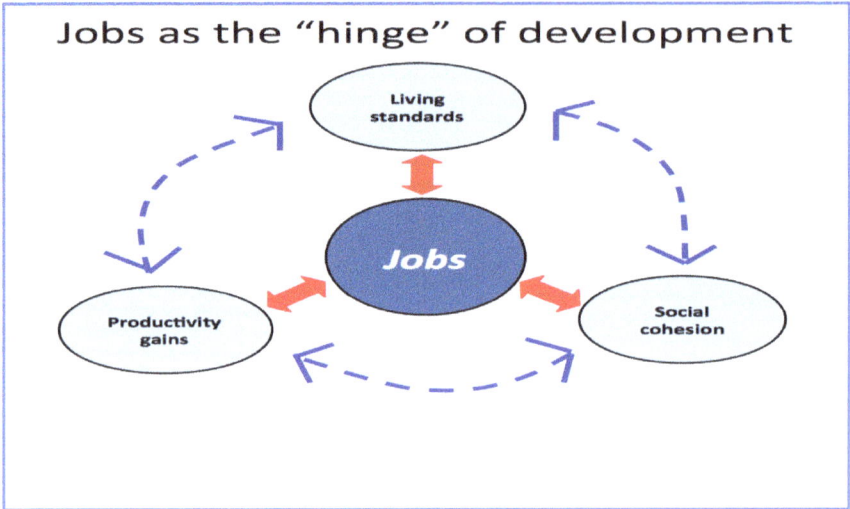

Figure 2.4.

The above discussion reminds us that well-functioning labor markets are a pre-requisite for households to allocate sufficient time for income-earning activities. But, such markets are nearly absent in rural South Sudan where more than 80% of the population lives [World Bank, 2013]. Note that in a post-conflict economy such as South Sudan, and especially in the rural parts of the country, job creation may be seriously stymied by the absence of effective demand on the part of consumers and firms. Rural South Sudan suffers from under-consumption arising from the absence of liquidity. Recognizing that, job creation might plausibly be jump-started by the careful introduction of liquidity into the economy. Think of it as "priming the pump." Such liquidity would immediately stimulate a variety of important market activities. In post-conflict settings, and this is especially true in South Sudan—which had a seriously under-developed economy before the conflict started in the 1980s—the pressing need is to begin to get money circulating again in rural areas.

While jobs raise living standards of those who manage to obtain jobs, it is also essential to keep in mind the profound income multipliers associated with consumer and producer purchases. In the short run, gradual infusions of liquidity will lift aggregate demand in the rural areas of South Sudan. At the present time there is simply so little money to be spent. As long as there is little effective demand (liquidity) in an economy, it will be impossible to bring about a real recovery.

IV. Jobs and Social Cohesion

The most important challenge facing post-conflict societies is to reinvigorate the sense of belonging to a community. In the early days of independence, social cohesion around the idea of the "new South Sudan" was not a problem. Nine years on from independence, it is difficult to claim a similar sense of social cohesion. Indeed, South Sudan is on a knife's edge. If economic recovery does not soon get underway, the euphoria of nationhood will give way to the frustration of idleness and the absence of hope. There is a danger of a "revolution of rising expectations." Frustrated aspirations—seemingly within reach—can become dangerous if not rectified.

The obvious danger arises because there are a number of ethnic communities that increasingly valorize their own identities and aspirations now that the former common enemy (the "North") is no longer the threat it once had been. This reminds us that improved livelihoods—

jobs—are the cornerstone not just of economic progress but of the necessary social cohesion that provides the essential "glue" for the idea of a nation-state to take hold. We see the necessary emphasis for donors and the government being concerned with creating enhanced livelihood prospects for all communities. Out of many there must become one. That is what nation building entails.

Our focus here on social cohesion pertains to how jobs can create and strengthen social cohesion. To elaborate, there are two general notions at work. The first, from the Council of Europe, defines social cohesion as "society's ability to secure the long-term well-being of all its members, including equitable access to available resources, respect for human dignity with due regard for diversity, personal and collective autonomy and responsible participation" [Council of Europe, 2005, p. 23]. The second notion is from the OECD [2012] which conceptualizes social cohesion as composed of three major components: (1) social inclusion; (2) social capital; and (3) social mobility.

Considering the above two definitions, social cohesion is the inherent sense of togetherness in the face of events and shocks beyond the control of the individual and/or community. Stated differently, it is the ability of autonomous well-informed individuals in a pluralistic society to create a space for one another to belong under the atmosphere of reciprocal respect and trustworthiness, with passion in non-confrontational civic/communal engagement for the promotion of their long-term well-being and upward social mobility.

Social scientists have long studied the concept of social cohesion in different contexts. This work started with the French sociologist Émile Durkheim (1858-1917) and his focus on the effects of modernization and industrialization on community solidarity. In contemporary settings, economists study social cohesion in an attempt to understand how institutions (laws, customs, habitual practices) contribute to overall economic well-being. Political scientists such as Putnam [1993] seek to understand the correlation between social cohesion and the effectiveness of service delivery, accountability, and tendencies toward democratic values. Psychologists tend to worry about how relationships within a group affect individual social outcomes such as health, education and social status. Some scholars [Chipkin & Ngqulunga 2008; Jenson, 1998; Kearns & Forrest, 2000; Putnam, 1993] argue that affective bond (e.g. culture, social organizations, and reciprocity) among citizens brings them together in cohesive communities.

Trust and reciprocity seem to be the key drivers of social cohesion and are consistent with the three attributes—inclusion, capital, and mobility—in the definition of the OECD. In this regard, Putnam's work is in line with one of the elements of the OECD definition. It is mainly about social capital in which networks of civic engagement (i.e. associated norms of reciprocity and trustworthiness) do matter [Putnam, 2007]. Social capital is about informal norms that promote "co-operation between two or more individuals" [Fukuyama, 2001; p. 7]. But it is not every trust that matters. The personalized or particularized trust—that which is limited to people personally known—has a very limited relationships to productivity and social cohesion [Stolle, 1998]. This reminds us that meaningful social cohesion refers to other-regarding behavior that necessarily *reaches beyond* known persons. It must, if it is to be meaningful, extend to the "other." In the absence of reaching "others" we end up with family-clan-club-church affinities which are not extensive enough. They simply recapitulate existing social enclaves. Indeed, as we reflect on the long and tragic civil war between the two Sudans, the struggle was about strict conceptions by the majority in the former Sudan that precipitated the rejection that led to the creation of South Sudan. It is important that the new country of South Sudan not descend into the minefield that swallowed up the former Sudan.

Recalling the opening quote in Chapter 1 from the philosopher Richard Rorty, moral progress is increasing sensitivity to the interests of larger and larger communities of others. Moreover, the trust that contributes to economic coherence and improved productivity must be generalized trust "which extends beyond the boundaries of face-to-face interaction" [Stolle, 1998; p.503]. Uslaner [2010] argues that generalized

41

trust means accepting strangers in our moral community. Lack of such acceptance is parasitic on economic productivity and therefore undermines precarious long-term gains in living standards. Miguel [2004] has found that low inter-ethnic cooperation in Kenya led to reductions in school investment. That is, most parents refused to engage in fundraising for their ethnically diverse school because of durable rivalries. Social cohesion, or the lack thereof—is parasitic on progress.

Lower trust is also associated with economic inequality [Knack, 2003]. Hjort [2014] found that inter-ethnic rivalry following election violence in 2008 reduced allocative efficiency in Kenya. National programs that reach all ethnicities equally can increase generalized trust [Rothstein, 2005]. While certain jobs presumably create social cohesion among distinct social elements, the nature of pre-existing element-specific groups' relations can impede this desired harmony. Hjort [2014] has explored the influence of ethnic disparities on firm-level productivity between two Kenyan rival ethnic groups (Kikuyu and Luo). Results suggest that the level of productivity falls under ethnically heterogeneous teams, and increases under ethnically homogeneous teams.

In the African context, the most relevant case of "social cohesion engineering" is that of Julius Nyerere's Tanzania. This initiative was anchored on the conviction of President Nyerere that: "In our traditional African society we were individuals within a community. We took care of the community, and the community took care of us. We neither needed nor wished to exploit our fellow men [Nyerere, 1966]." President Nyerere had conceptualized *Ujamaa* as his development blueprint, which became popularly known as the Arusha Declaration. The point of relevance for South Sudan is the possibility of reinvigorating the sense of belonging to a community through an "African model of development" rooted in African socialism [Nyerere, 1966]. We must caution, however, that the *Ujamaa* experiment has been subjected to criticism. It is still useful, we believe, to unpack what was in play there.

Using Nyerere's framework, social cohesion can be examined at three critical levels. The first level is the macro-level (national level) where a call for social cohesion is synonymous with a nation-building project. What matters at the national level is not the nature of jobs but rather the context (or environment) in which such jobs exist and are created. Here the key characteristics of social inclusion and social mobility become paramount for those willing to undertake economic activity anywhere in their nation-state. The economist W. Arthur Lewis considers economic activity as "the will to make the human efforts to increase the yield of a given effort or resource [1955, p. 23]." This "will," is largely constrained under weak and fragile social cohesion and could easily lead into "limited horizons" and consequently frustrations, followed by anti-social values and norms. Social cohesion would therefore become one of the key drivers, at the macro-level, of jobs that in turn raise living standards as well as increase productivity growth. If countries can get the quest for social cohesion right, productivity growth will take care of itself and consequently create a robust demand for jobs that raise living standards.

The desire for social cohesion at the meso-level is somewhat complicated. Here we encounter various communities and ethnic-based administrative units/territories. The Kikuyu-Luo rivalry in Kenya, and the Dinka-Murle-Nuer cattle rustling in Jonglei State of South Sudan, are examples at this level. The sense of belonging to a particular ethnic-based/defined community is still very strong and it is more influenced by micro-level factors/variables than by the macro-level (national) ones. For instance, insecure livelihoods are more closely felt at the micro-level (household), since this impinges on what Lewis calls "the desire for goods." Moreover, communities that place a high premium on "wealth and social status" will place additional burdens on households to embark on the process of wealth accumulation that might not always be consistent with the fundamentals of social cohesion.

The third level (micro-level) of jobs and social cohesion is the household. To Lewis, "growth of output per head depends on the one hand on natural resources available, and on the other hand on human behaviour" [1955, p. 10]. These references guide our search to understand the primary factors/variables that are likely to undermine social

43

cohesion at the meso- and macro-levels of South Sudan. The behavior of households in the utilization of resources (including time) at their disposal is a critical factor in any meaningful analysis of the quality of livelihoods—and by extension, living standards.

It is important to understand that the kinds of ethnic rivalry discussed above can plausibly be traced to the ever-present threat of insecure livelihoods. Recall that livelihood stresses—"household" security—tend to bring out the very kind of self-regarding behavior that undermines social cohesion. For instance, if an individual's livelihood prospects are tenuous, that individual will be most likely to retreat into a defensive mode of behavior to preserve the relative well-being of the family. As the general economy begins to pick up, and if it then becomes apparent that "others" are less of a threat to future livelihood prospects, then the individual can relax and perhaps become more open to the "other." The point here is that discussions of social cohesion must avoid the notion that ethnic tension is some immutable part of Kikuyu and Luo (or Dinka, Murle, and Nuer) DNA. These tensions arise because of existing livelihood insecurities. When livelihoods are more secure, much of the reason for suspicion of the "other" will disappear.

This brings us back to the role of the state in the creation of an enabling environment for jobs that enhance social cohesion. The necessary purpose of the state and its government is to keep working hard to improve—to secure—all livelihoods. Over time, ethnic tensions will begin to dissipate. This should not reduce to a discussion of the brute notion of material greed. Rather, we here encounter the idea of safety-first for one's family [Day and Singh, 1977].

For instance, the feeling of economic marginalization—particularly in France—fuels part of the ethnic tension we see in Europe. Immigrants from North Africa and the Middle East are blamed for a variety of ficti-tious perils. On the other hand, Germany has a long history of tolerance for its Turkish millions. The difference has its roots in material conditions. Following World War II, West Germany faced a severe labor shortage. Turkish *Gastarbeiters* (guest workers) were welcomed because they filled an important economic need, and they did not compete with locals for jobs. It is impossible to say that there are labor shortages in much of Europe today. And hence immigrants—others—are a clear threat to many workers. We see a "materialist" link between livelihoods (jobs) and social cohesion. It works in the manufacturing of German automobiles, and it works in the raising of cattle in the Nile Basin. Some things are rather "universal." Livelihoods are universal needs and sources of stress.

Social capital, social inclusion and social mobility are the fundamental pillars of social cohesion. Unfortunately, in South Sudan, these pillars have been weakened if not destroyed during the long violent conflict against Sudan. South Sudan is starting from a very low level of social capital, lower trust, and generally restrained reciprocity. These attributes are the cause, and the effect, of insecurity over livelihoods. They lead to ethnic tension and hostility.

As a second point, it is not the nature of jobs that enhances social cohesion. Rather, the general environment, with a supportive climate for the "will to make the human effort," provides the conditions that can enhance jobs, productivity, and rising living standards. The challenge, therefore, is to nurture the enabling environment for jobs that are likely to enhance social cohesion, and also to raise living standards.

A third point concerns the idea that jobs are the essential "hinge" of development. Such a presupposition is somewhat more tenuous in a post-conflict setting faced with the cumulative consequences of a long violent conflict. In this regard, it must be kept in mind that South Sudan is not just a "typical post-conflict society." It is at one extreme on a continuum containing dozens of countries. Yet, we insist that there is a causal nexus between jobs and enhanced social cohesion. With that as a maintained hypothesis, the GRSS must take the lead in a comprehensive effort to strengthen that nexus. This necessary initiative requires an enabling environment in which most citizens see that the general tide is rising and "lifting most boats"—differentially, perhaps, but lifting them, nonetheless.

Nyerere's model of nation building through development supports this point about the need for the government to be the active agent in creating trust so that the "differential lifting of boats" in these early days will be "evened out" in the fullness of time.

V. Implications

The creation of a *real economy* in South Sudan, a future beyond oil, must be the paramount priority of the government. That commitment will require specific attention be paid to several key attributes of the economy: (1) the legal parameters associated with land and land-use; (2) food security and agricultural development; (3) job creation in the private sector to bolster sustainable livelihoods; and (4) creation of a viable system of public-service provision throughout the country. Those themes will be addressed in subsequent chapters.

REFERENCES

Bromley, Daniel W. 1989. *Economic Interests and Institutions: The Conceptual Foundations of Public Policy*, Oxford: Blackwell.

Bromley, Daniel W. 2006. *Sufficient Reason: Volitional Pragmatism and the Meaning of Economic Institutions*, Princeton: Princeton University Press.

Bromley, Daniel W. 2008. "Resource Degradation in the African Commons: Accounting for Institutional Decay," *Environment and Development Economics*, 13:539-63.

Bromley, Daniel W. and Glen D. Anderson. 2012. *Vulnerable People, Vulnerable States: Redefining the Development Challenge*, London: Routledge.

Chipkin, I. and B. Ngqulunga, B. 2008. "Friends and Family: Social Cohesion in South Africa," *Journal of Southern African Studies*, 34:61-76.

Council of Europe. 2005. Concerted Developments of Social Cohesion Indicators: Methodological Guide, Strasbourg: Council of Europe Publishing.

Day, Richard and Inderjit Singh. 1977. *Economic Development as an Adaptive Process: A Green Revolution Case Study*, Cambridge: Cambridge University Press.

Deng, Lual, Nada Omer Eisa, Daniel W. Bromley, James A. Garang, Anthony Harris, Augustino T. Mayai, and Zechariah M. Biar. 2012. South Sudan: Creating Jobs for Sustained Peace, Economic Growth and Poverty Reduction. a Report of the *Case Study on Jobs* for the World Development Report

Easterly, William. 2001. "Can Institutions Resolve Ethnic Conflict?" Economic Development and Cultural Change, 49(4):687–706.

Easterly, William and Ross Levine. 2001. "It's not factor accumulation: Stylized facts and growth models," The World Bank Economic Review, 15:177–219.

Fukuyama, F. 2001. "Social capital, civil society and development." Third World Quarterly, 22:7-20.

Hjort, J. 2014. "Ethnic Divisions and Production in Firms," *Quarterly Journal of Economics*, 129(4):1899-1946.

Jenson, J. 1998. *Mapping Social Cohesion: The State of Canadian Research*. Ontario: Canadian Policy Research Networks.

Kaldor, Nicholas. 1961. "Capital Accumulation and Economic Growth." In F.A. Lutz and D.C. Hague, eds. *The Theory of Capital*, London: St.Martins Press, pp. 177–222.

Kearns, A., & Forrest, R. 2000. "Social Cohesion and Multilevel Urban Governance," *Urban Studies*, 37: 995-1017.

Knack, S. 2003. "Groups, growth, and trust: Cross-country evidence on the Olson and Putnam hypotheses," *Public Choice*, 117:341-355.

Lewis, W. Arthur. 1955. *The Theory of Economic Growth*, London: Allen and Unwin.

Mack, Andrew. 2002. "Civil War: Academic Research and the Policy Community," *Journal of Peace Research*, 39:515–525.

Miguel, E. 2004. "Tribe or Nation? Nation Building and Public Goods in Kenya versus Tanzania," *World Politics*, 56:327–62.

Nyerere, Julius K. 1966. *Freedom and Unity*, Oxford: Oxford University Press.

OECD. 2012. *Perspectives on Global Development 2012: Social Cohesion in a Shifting World*, OECD Publishing. Paris.

Prebisch, Raul. 1962. "The Economic Development of Latin America and its Principal Problems," *Economic Bulletin for Latin America*, 7:1-22.

Putnam, Robert. 1993. *Making Democracy Work: Civic Traditions in Modern Italy*. Princeton: Princeton University Press.

Putman, Robert. 1995. "Bowling Alone: America's Declining Social Capital." *Journal of Democracy*, 6: 65-78.

Putnam, Robert. 2007. "E Pluribus Unum: Diversity and Community in the Twenty-first Century." *Scandinavian Political Studies*, 30:137-174.

Rothstein, B. 2005. *Social Traps and the Problem of Trust*, Cambridge: Cambridge University Press.

Schiavo-Campo, Salvatore and Daniel Tommasi. 1999. *Managing Government Expenditure*, Manila: Asian Development Bank.

Steger, Thomas. 2001. "Stylised facts of economic growth in developing countries." Discussion Paper Ernst-Moritz-Arndt University of Greifswald. Discussion Paper 08, 2001.

Stolle, D. 1998. "Bowling Together, Bowling Alone: The Development of Generalized Trust in Voluntary Associations," *Political Psychology*, 19: 497-525.

Uslaner, E. M. 2010. *The Moral Foundations of Trust*, Cambridge: Cambridge University Press.

World Bank. 2013. *World Development Report 2013: Jobs*. Washington, D.C.

CHAPTER 3

The Legal Foundations of Sustainable Livelihoods:
Achieving Peace and Economic Development Through Land Reforms

Santino Ayuel Longar

I. Introduction

In 2011, the Republic of the (Old) Sudan split into two sovereign nations namely; the Republic of South Sudan and the Republic of the Sudan. The split of the then Africa's largest country by landmass came on the heels of many decades of an on-and-off civil war,[2] dubbed in the then

---

2   The first civil war between Southern and Northern Sudan started in 1955. This war ended when the Anya Nya I Movement—made of Southern Sudanese, signed an agreement with the Northern Sudan's dominated Government Jaafar Mohamed el Nimeiry in 1972. The Agreement lasted only for 10 years before el Nimeiry abrogated in 1982, leading to the formation of SPLM/A in 1983. The SPLM/A would later sign the Comprehensive Peace Agreement (CPA) with the Sudan's junta Government of Omar el Bashir in 2005. This CPA paved way for the Referendum that allowed the people of South Sudan to overwhelming vote for independence on January 9, in 2011.

Southern Sudan as a *war of liberation*. The final phase of the war began in 1983, following the May 16 Bor mutiny that preceded the formation of the Sudan Peoples' Liberation Movement/Army (SPLM/A) led by its late leader, Chairman John Garang de Mabior. The SPLM/A would subsequently prosecute a vicious war with various Khartoum governments for 21 years until both sides signed the Comprehensive Peace Agreement (CPA) on January 9, 2005. The 21-year long South-North war saw an almost total destruction of economic, political and social structures across Southern Sudan.

At independence on July 9, 2011, thus, South Sudan inherited enormous institutional and structural weaknesses that continue to undercut its ability to consolidate its independence and statehood. Furthermore, the sudden rise in political tensions from within the ruling SPLM soon after independence culminated in an outbreak of violence on December 15, 2013. This violence launched what became known as South Sudan's First Civil War. This war pitted Government forces against those loyal to the current First Vice President, Riek Machar. It quickly transformed itself into a brutal conflict, claiming at least tens of thousands of South Sudanese lives. Here the phrase "at least" is a caveat, having regard to the fact that other studies estimate the war fatalities to be as high as 400,000 over a period of 5 years—from 2013 to 2018 [Rolandsen, 2015; de Wal, 2015; *The Sentry Report*, 2019; London School of Hygiene and Tropical Medicine, 2018].[3]

In September 2018, the international community pressured major parties to the conflict into signing the Revitalized Agreement on the Resolution of the Conflict in the Republic of South Sudan (R-ARCSS). The R-ARCSS seemingly heralded a new beginning for the world's youngest country through structural and institutional reforms. In keeping with the scheme and spirit of the R-ARCSS, as well as the South Sudanese people's aspirations for a better country and future, thus, this chapter examines the legal foundations of sustainable

---

3   While a number of Western studies put the number of fatalities at almost 400,000, this figure is largely contested—especially in South Sudan.

livelihoods, with specific attention to necessary land reforms stipulated in the R-ARCSS.

Prior to examining the question of land reforms, the chapter devotes itself to a brief discussion of the centrality of the state—that is, a government and its associated political community—in providing opportunities for sustainable livelihoods. That is, the existence of a coherent state is a condition precedent for the citizens of South Sudan to secure for themselves the necessary opportunities for achieving sustainable livelihoods. This proposition is self-evident in light of the fact that the state is responsible for the security and the provision of assorted necessities of life. In other words, the concept of sustainable livelihoods presupposes the existence of a prudent and proactive South Sudanese state with the capacity to provide a conducive environment within which citizens may then engage in productive activities—thereby enjoying a more dignified existence [Dimitrovska, 2015; Thompson, 1995; Ayoob, 2002].

The second portion of the chapter analyzes the significance of sustainable livelihoods in the context of land reforms. It is noteworthy that the vast majority of land ownership is under the control of indigenous communities which generally entails the shared jurisdiction of traditional authorities and the government's major constituent units—states and administrative areas. Of great importance, the political and economic significance that land has gained in recent years means that land disputes have become a source of explosive conflicts—both between local government authorities (states and administrative areas) and various ethnic communities. In that connection, the chapter seeks to offer an approach by which the Government might consider dealing with the issue of clarifying internal boundaries as they stood on January 1, 1956.

Furthermore, because of the absence of a clear and definitive public land policy—combined with the contentious internal borders that lurk behind the cycles of violence that have arisen since 2013—the chapter will also suggest that a binding determination of internal (ethnic and administrative) boundaries would have a salutary effect in mitigating the frequency and severity of ethnic and interjurisdictional conflicts. Such a determination could also mitigate the severity of systemic destructive practices such as land grabbing and fraudulent land transactions. These palliative measures would enhance the climate for private investments in land, thereby increasing the productive use of land.

In an effort to mitigate the severity of land disputes and border conflicts, the R-ARCSS created the Technical Boundaries Committee (TBC) to define and demarcate ethnic boundaries as they stood on January 1, 1956. This activity is as much intended to mitigate the severity of land disputes as it is to serve the cause of peace and thereby promote sustainable livelihoods and encourage economic development.

II. The Legal Foundations of Sustainable Livelihood

As part of concerted efforts to encourage the people of South Sudan to embrace lasting peace, and to pursue opportunities for sustainable livelihoods and economic development, the role of the government as a prudent manager of public resources is indispensable. A government that satisfies its responsibility to maintain law and order also comes to enjoy considerable legitimacy in the eyes of its citizens. Effective states require honest and effective governments.

The literature is clear that international law does not vest absolute sovereignty in governments [Deng, et al, 1996; Cohen & Deng, 1998; Macklem, 2015; Fox-Decent, 2011]. This reminds us that sovereignty is contingent upon the ability of the government to meet its empirical responsibilities towards its citizens. Coherent states have governments that acknowledge their duties to citizens. This responsibility is a function of an obligation to protect the rights and freedoms of all its citizens. The restraint on sovereignty enables the government to make laws and maintain the peace. At the same time, this restraint ensures that citizens enjoy an innate prerogative to censure the exercise of governmental authority. This trade-off constrains the government's behavior and thereby cushions citizens from injuries that arise from excesses of the exercise of sovereign authority [Macklem, 2015, p. 105].

The legal foundations of sustainable livelihoods, therefore, presupposes a well-functioning state [Hinsch and Stepanians, 2005, Martin, 2013; Duruigbo, 2008]. In other words, an efficacious state is endowed with the legal, institutional, and financial ability to deal with a wide range of issues that include the promotion of human development, protection of civil liberties, and the provision of essential goods and services at all levels of society [Dimitrovska, 2015]. This makes the nation-state the universal medium of international relations and the formulation of global policies [Thompson, 1995]. The nation-state is, therefore, a fiduciary of its people's welfare.

The common law concept of fiduciary generally regulates the relationship between two parties in which a *trust property* is managed or administered by another party, called the *fiduciary* (in whom legal title is vested) for the benefit of a dependent[4] party, called *beneficiary* (in whom an equitable title is vested). A fiduciary exercises discretionary authority in the administration of the trust property within reasonable legal constraints [Fox-Decent, 2011].

Evan Fox-Decent situates the government's fiduciary responsibilities in a constitutional context that defines the relationship between the government and its subjects. This relationship undergirds both the authority of the government and its political entities to make laws, and it ensures that the government exercises its obligations within the limits of the rule of law. This dual relationship must be flexible enough to enable a government to provide a judicial system that guarantees the legal rights of all its subjects [Fox-Decent, 2011]. The government must treat every subject or citizen as an end and not as an instrument for the government's desired end. Construed as such, the idea of sustainable livelihoods imposes a positive duty upon the government to protect the well-being

---

4   A beneficiary is normally regarded as "vulnerable" because he or she is under some form of disability (such as being elderly, a minor, or disabled).

of its subjects and create a peaceful environment within which citizens are able to secure opportunities with which to improve their welfare [Kant, 1991]. The problem at the present time is that the government of South Sudan remains unable to fulfill its responsibilities to create a conducive environment for sustainable livelihoods.

III. Sustainable Livelihoods: A Conceptual Framework

The concept of sustainable livelihoods underscores the need for societal efforts to use human and economic resources to improve the material conditions of all people, especially of the most vulnerable members of society [Serrat, 2020].

In this vein, an approach to sustainable livelihoods seeks to organize or regulate factors that either constrain or advance the cause of livelihood opportunities. It also underlines how these factors intimately relate to one another. For this reason, a proper ordering of factors of sustainable livelihoods examines a realistic assessment of the contribution that human activities make in a given socio-economic environment. It also facilitates the process of identifying practical priorities for human action. This implies an emphasis on the inherent human potential in the forms of skills, social networks, and resources that determine ultimate outcomes and decision-making within essential government entities. As such, human capabilities and material assets needed to improve human conditions are imperatives of securing sustainable livelihood opportunities [Serrat, 2020].

It stands to reason that an approach to sustainable livelihoods is consistent with the protection of human welfare or *needs*. All human beings, by their very nature, have scientifically ascertainable needs that the law must strive to protect and promote [Donnelly, 1985, 2013]. It is for this reason that the concept of sustainable livelihoods is enshrined both in international and municipal laws. For instance, in order to secure sustainable livelihoods for the people of South Sudan, the 2011

Transitional Constitution of the Republic of South Sudan (TCSS), as well as international human rights instruments, underscore the primacy of protecting natural resources.

The Preamble of the TCSS stipulates that the people of South Sudan are "conscious of the need of managing their natural resources *sustainably* and efficiently for the benefit of the present and future generations and to eradicate poverty and attain Millennium Development Goals." Article 36 (d) of TCSS is even more specific in providing that the people of South Sudan are ready, willing and able to mobilize their energies and resources in their collective quest for reconstructing and developing their country. Article 37 (b) places a positive duty on the Government at all levels to take practical measures to enhance means of "sustainable management and utilization of natural resources, including land, water, petroleum, minerals, fauna and flora for the benefit of the people."

Similarly, Article 41 (c) of TCSS seeks "to secure ecologically sustainable development and use of natural resources while promoting rational economic and social development so as to protect genetic stability and bio-diversity." This view is even clearer in Article 38 (b) which commits the government to "mobilize public, private and communal resources and capabilities for education and promotion of scientific research geared towards development." Along the same line, Article 157 (b) mandates the government to "manage wildlife resources in a manner that will ensure the protection of human life."

The legal foundations of sustainable livelihoods are also supported by international instruments. For instance, Article 1 (2) of the International Covenant on Economic, Social and Cultural Rights (ICESCR) states that "all people may, for their own ends, freely dispose of their natural wealth and resources without prejudice to any obligations arising out of international economic cooperation, based upon the principle of mutual benefit, and international law. In no case may a people be deprived of its own means of subsistence."

Article 2 (1) of the same instrument also commits every States Party to the Covenant to takes practical steps, both individually and through international cooperation and assistance whether economic and technical "to the maximum available resources, with the view to achieving progressively the full realization of the rights recognized in the Present Covenant by all appropriate means, including particularly the adoption of legislative measures."

In the same vein, Article 11 (2) (a) of ICESCR mandates States Parties to the Covenant to not only recognize that every human person has the right to be free from hunger and poverty but also to, individually and through international cooperation, initiate specific programs that are necessary for enhancing means of production, conservation and distribution of resources as well as reforming agrarian systems. All this aims at achieving the most efficient utilization and development of natural resources, and promotion of opportunities for sustainable livelihoods in society.

Furthermore, the scheme, purpose, and spirit of the R-ARCSS offers the Republic of South Sudan an opportunity to reboot itself. With respect to the political and economic significance that land has gained in South Sudan in recent years, the following section underscores the importance of institutional reforms in general—and land reforms in particular.

A. Securing Peace and Sustainable Livelihoods Through Land Reforms

Although the R-ARCSS did not bring on board all warring forces in the country, its signing paved the way for the formation of the current Revitalized Transitional Government of National Unity (RTGONU) in February 2020. The RTGONU's formation followed several delays as parties could not agree on a number of Pre-transitional issues including the number and boundaries of states.

Under Chapter IV, the R-ARCSS prescribes far-reaching reforms. These include the creation of a transparent and accountable system of government. Such a government must be guided by an unwavering pursuit of, and commitment to, sustainable livelihoods and development.

It also envisions a political environment in which the leadership commits itself to: (1) fighting corruption; (2) developing a rigid code of ethics and high moral standards on the part of public officials; (3) promoting values of honesty, integrity and competence; and (4) establishing oversight procedures pertaining to the collection and allocation of revenues and budgeting/expenditure. As well, the reform agenda calls for an equitable sharing of resources at various levels of government. All this would be undertaken in liaison with the international community.

While the Preamble to the R-ARCSS actually aspires to create a federal system that reflects ethnic and regional diversity, the reform agenda seeks to promote a decentralized system of governance. At first blush, Chapter IV, which prioritizes decentralization, may seem at variance with the other provisions on the need for a federal system of government. However, the idea of decentralization under Chapter IV specifically refers to the need for establishing multiple centers of decision-making, particularly on matters pertaining to development and service delivery. There is no contradiction, thus, in R-ARCISS calling for a federal system that reflects ethnic and regional diversity and, also committing the parties to adopt a decentralized system of government.

The following section will focus on the structural aspects of land reforms, land management, and land administration. This emphasis acknowledges that land and border conflicts have become increasingly contentious. This contention arises from the fact that, as South Sudan's population grows and puts more pressure on land and related resources, the economic significance and, therefore, demand for land will necessarily increase. Furthermore, the burgeoning economic significance of land has, in turn, led to a scramble for land especially among those with influence (in terms of political power and wealth). Their aim is to amass more land and resources, both for themselves and, to some extent, their political and ethnic constituencies. Obviously, this behavior has led to more land disputes and conflicts over borders [Forojalla and Galla, 2010].

The R-ARCSS contains elaborate provisions on land policy and administration. Chapter IV, paragraphs 4.8.2.1.1 to 4.8.2.1.4, specific commits the R-TGONU to take measures relating to land policy and administration. It mandates the R-TGONU to initiate, within 12 months of the commencement of the Transitional Period, an in-depth nation-wide debate to review the 2008 South Sudan Land Act. The purpose of this review would be to seek consensus with respect to land reforms—especially with respect to land tenure, land use and management as well as mapping. This review process has not yet begun. The reforms agenda also seeks to eradicate systemic malpractices such as land grabbing and fraudulent transactions involving land. More importantly, the Chapter mandates the RTGONU to undertake internal land mapping.

Furthermore, within 18 months of the commencement of the Transitional Period, the reform provisions mandate the establishment of an independent Lands Registry at all levels of Government. The Registry would ensure that correct land titles/deeds are issued to rightful land owners. Finally, the reform provisions empower land commissions, at all levels of government, to develop legislation that incorporates the relevance and significance of various customary land laws, local practices, and institutional procedures essential for mediating land disputes. The land mapping exercise should also include the determination of internal borders. Such a determination would mitigate the on-going issue of land disputes.

B. The Centrality of the State in Land Policy and Administration

The fundamentals of public land policy and administration generally revolve around the issue of whether land is being regulated and managed equitably. An equitable regulation of land occurs when existing institutional arrangements—laws and administrative procedures—are just and reasonably tailored to promoting societal and individual welfare [Barlowe, 1972; Qadeer, 1985]. Those policies and procedures ensure that land is allocated, regulated, and managed fairly and equitably. In this regard, the government has the sole responsibility and authority to undertake structural land reforms, and to make decisions that are binding on all actors within its sovereign jurisdiction—citizens and non-citizens alike.

The instrumentality of the government in matters pertaining to land reforms springs from the idea that respect for the rule of law is necessary and that chaos is inimical to the principles of a fair, just, and a well-ordered society. Every society, whether large or small, powerful or weak, should establish a set of legal principles with which it regulates land management and administration. This authority expresses itself in the form of the government having to pass legislation that constitutes a central part of sustainable land policy and administration. The rule of law—rather than the rule of elites or *ad hoc* responses to events— is imperative in the process of land reforms [Gilroy and Sim, 1985, *Roncarelli v. Duplessis,* 1959].

Against the background of recent civil conflicts, coupled with its recent independence, South Sudan is institutionally weak. Its government is hampered in its ability to competently deal with the range of issues such as: (1) land grabbing; (2) the unilateral redrawing of boundaries by local governors or vice presidents; (3) the lack of clear internal boundaries; (4) land-disputes management; and (5) an ineffective land-registration and titling system.

The process of acquiring, managing and owning land in South Sudan is, thus, fraught with major difficulties. For instance, in a Technical Workshop conducted by the National Dialogue in February, 2020, many participants raised serious concerns about the ubiquity of irregularities in land management and administration.[5] These concerns include: (1) questionable practices such as extra-judicial collection of land registration fees; (2) overlapping issuance of land titles to multiple purchasers—particularly in urban areas such as Juba; and (3) legitimization of mass land theft (land grabbing). This situation is further exacerbated by the government's inability to effectively manage and

---

5   Led by the author, the workshop was conducted in Juba from February 24 to 25, 2020, under the auspices of South Sudan's National Dialogue and partners.

settle land disputes between communities and other competing tenure holders [Deng, 2014]. To overcome some of these difficulties, the government should launch practical steps towards a more coherent and effective land policy and regulatory structure.

Land management and administration in South Sudan is generally founded on the principles of popular and broad-based participation. For instance, Section 41 (2) of the Land Act states that prior to any decision being taken, relevant regulatory authorities must consult with traditional leaders and local governments—as well as particularly communities who are affected by such decisions. Despite this legal specificity, land management and administration often take different approaches.

IV. Forms of Land Ownership in South Sudan

Despite the fact that the TCSS, pursuant to Article 171 (4) and (7), vests absolute management and regulation of subterranean natural resources in the Government, land ownership, use and a management in South Sudan take three forms namely; *public, private* and *community* lands.

A. Public Land

Public land refers to any piece of land held or acquired for public use or that which is reserved for public programs such as environmental and wildlife protection [Outka, 2017, pp. 166-7; Department of the Interior, 2016, p.255]. Both the TCSS and the Land Act codify the concept of public land within the meaning the Colonial Ordinances bequeathed to the Sudan by colonial authorities in the twentieth century. Today, the TCSS (Article 171 (3) and Land Act (Article 10 (2)) prescribe the scope of public land to all types of land acquired or held by any level of government in South Sudan.

However, Article 10 (2) of the Land Act is much broader than the constitutional provision of Article 171 (3). Article 10 (2) defines public land as any piece of land acquired by or transferred to any level of government (local, state and central), or land which the government acquires by way of reversion or surrender, or any land in relation to which no heir is entitled to acquire, either directly or indirectly. Under the same article, the definition of public land includes physical infrastructures such as roads, airspace, railways, rivers, lakes, airports as well as thoroughfare, water catchment areas or such other property as the law may prescribe, insofar as no customary ownership can be established. Public land also covers game reserves and forests as well as recreational facilities legally designated as public properties. This suggests that there is no such thing as a "no-man's land" in South Sudan [Julius, 2015].

B. Community Land

The single largest form of land ownership in South Sudan is community land which simply describes any land acquired by or held in the name of the community. Such a collective ownership suggests that only the community has the ability to use, allocate or transfer interests in any piece of land designated as community land. It is for this reason that only the community in which land is vested has the prerogative to regulate access rights for all community members as well as for outsiders. This also suggests that while freehold tenure is vested in the community, outsiders can only acquire land tenure by way of leasehold. This also means that outsiders are only allowed limited access to community land. Freehold tenure grants land owners the right to own land or interests in land perpetually, whereas leasehold tenure allows the land owner to use land for a specific period of time. Following the expiry of the agreed-upon period, the leaseholder may renew the lease. Otherwise, the land or interests in land revert to the original owner [Andersen, 2011].

Finally, Article 4 of the Land Act refers to community land as any land "owned or controlled by a family, clan or a designated community leader" while Article 11 (1) and (2) of the same Act defines community land as any land that communities hold on the basis of ethnic identity, residence or interest. The constitutional provision of Article 170 (5) defines community land as any land historically held or used by local communities. Because community land is regulated by communal customs in South Sudan, there are as many customs as there are communities. A more comprehensive public law is, thus, required to consolidate these fragmented land customs.

C. Private Land

Private land refers to any piece of land acquired or held either by a natural or corporate person. If the titleholder is the original owner, then that person holds it by way of freehold/fee simple which entitles the land owner the perpetual right of ownership that places fewer restrictions one's occupation or use [Merrill, 1998]. Where private land is held by way of an equitable title, it is terminally held by way of leasehold tenure. Upon expiry of the lease, the fee simple title or freehold automatically reverts to its original owner unless the lease is renewed [Feder & Feeny, 1991].

V. Limitations of The Forms of Land Ownership/ Classification

The tripartite classification of land in South Sudan is, however, highly problematic. For instance, private land ownership is quite vulnerable on three grounds. First, the problem of overlapping land ownership makes the security of private land tenure questionable. The term "overlapping" refers to several claims of ownership to the same parcel of land. In practice, overlapping occurs when a party sells—or seeks to sell—the same piece of land to several purchasers at different times. This issue is common in urban areas such as Juba where lack of an effective registration system makes it difficult for purchasers be certain who the authentic land owner is. The absence of title insurance compounds this problem. Furthermore, existing land laws and polices do not sufficiently articulate the legal authority that exercises jurisdiction over processes such as acquisition and registration. It is in this context that fraudulent transactions are quite prevalent in Juba. Once duped, there often is very little that a defrauded purchaser can do to mitigate his or her loss.

Similarly, the security of a community land regime is attenuated by lack of clear internal boundaries between counties and states across the country. That is because, whereas traditional communities know the limits of their boundaries, the burgeoning political and economic importance that land has gained in recent years has propelled influential political players to grab as much land as possible—often from their neighboring communities. The aim is to increase the economic and political influence of their own native constituencies. This occurs when public officials use their political power to forcefully annex their neighboring community's areas to their own constituencies. The net consequence is the ratcheting up of border conflicts across the country. Finally, conflicts over jurisdiction between the government and Traditional Authorities operate to undermine the security of community land tenure. This situation is exacerbated by the provision of Article 46 (a) of the Land Act which bestows on the government the prerogative of alienating or assigning rights in any *public land*, as long as such alienation is assented to by the relevant state ministry and municipal authorities. In practice, however, government authorities at all levels tend to usurp Traditional Authority's power to allocate or alienate interests in community land. The central government is now able, extrajudicially, to alienate all types of land (including community land).

The alienation of Traditional Authority from land governance in South Sudan is, perhaps a consequence of what Daniel Bromley refers to as culture of "possessive individualism" and that, in turn, engenders the "crisis of capitalism" [Bromley, 2019, see also Macpherson, 1962]. That is partly because modern capitalism seeks to promote structures that protect institutions of private property. This is clear from the fact that modern laws tends to draw clear legal boundaries between individual and collective ownership. In so doing, capitalist enterprise advances the interests of a few landholders [Pienaar, 2008].

Part of the solution to the issues that undermine the security of land tenure in South Sudan is three-fold. First, it is important to begin with the demarcation of internal boundaries. This can go a long way to mitigate the intensity of land and border disputes. Second, it is imperative that the government pass legislation on land reforms. These reforms should clearly limit the scope of the government's authority to allocate or alienate interests in land *to public land only*. Third, the ability of Traditional Authorities, under the Land Act (Article 15 (1) and (5), and Article. 27 (2) and (3), to allocate, manage, transfer or alienate interests in community land should be clarified and translated into a practical program. These provisions would confer on Traditional Authorities the power to regulate, manage and administer land concurrently, and in consultations, with the government.

Unfortunately, this concurrency suffers from two problems. First, as Forojolla and Galla observe, it remains unclear "how rights of different levels of government and communities and individuals, are defined in land held by government or traditionally held by communities" [Forojalla and Galla, 2010, p. A-5]. Second, Traditional Authorities are practically starved of financial resources. This means that incorporating Traditional Authorities into structures of land governance, when they are clearly toothless, leaves them vulnerable to being displaced by the other levels of the government. This circumstance leaves Traditional Authorities with very limited power to regulate and administer land concurrently with the government. Unfortunately, this means that decisions by Traditional Authorities are often overruled by the government.

For this and other reasons, the determination of internal boundaries as they stood on January 1st, 1956, is critical. This necessary specificity would further clarify the distinction between community and public lands.

VI. Determination of Internal Borders
as they stood on January 1, 1956

The determination of internal boundaries as they stood on January 1, 1956, is a practical requirement of Article 6 (4) of the Land Act which states that "all lands traditionally and historically held or used by local communities or their members shall be defined, held, managed and protected by law…." Article 11 (1) of the same Act also calls for the demarcation of community land based on but not limited to ethnicity, interests and residence. Article 8 (5) also operates to protect community land, while Article 39 requires a plaintiff community to adduce *prima facie* evidence as to the existence of communal land rights in the event of any conflict between the community and the government. Without translating the provisions of Article 6 (4) and 8 (5), as well as Article 11 (1), of the Land Act into practical land policy programs, Article 39 would be rendered redundant. Furthermore, the R-ARCSS (see page 23 of the 2018 Agreement) creates the Technical Boundary Committee (TBC) with the view to defining and demarcating tribal or ethnic boundaries of South Sudan as they stood on January 1, 1956. In this sense, the R-ARCSS seeks to settle the issue of border disputes arising from lack of clear internal borders.

It will be necessary, in order to demarcate internal boundaries, for the government to adopt specific legislation in this regard. But what sources of evidence should be used to precisely determine internal borders as they stood on January 1, 1956?

Customary laws and practices in South Sudan are largely fragmented, considering that each community has its own code of customs governing land management and administration. This fragmentation militates against any meaningful effort to consolidate and/or cross-fertilize customary laws with public laws. This, as well, makes it more difficult for various stakeholders to secure their respective interests in land. Yet, security of land tenure is important in light of its ability to improve opportunities for sustainable livelihoods.

The determination of internal boundaries is not just a requirement of the 2008 Land Act. It is also a popular demand. For instance, at an Upper Nile Regional Conference conducted by the South Sudan National Dialogue (May 20-25, 2019 in Juba), participants emphasized the distinction between two types of land—*rural* and urban *land.* Rural land, the Conference resolved, is that land which is owned by the community, whereas urban land refers to land that is both gazetted and vested in the government. The Conference also resolved that the government has the authority to lease and/or distribute (urban) land to individuals and organizations. More importantly, the Conference called upon the government to immediately and decisively resolve border disputes between feuding communities by demarcating internal borders [The National Dialogue, 2019, p. 3] as they stood on January 1, 1956.[6]

This regional call for the determination of internal boundaries is consistent with the scheme and spirit of the Land Act. For instance, Article 6 (4) of Land Act provides that "all lands traditionally and historically held or used by local communities or their members shall be defined, held, managed and protected by law...." Article 8 (6) further provides that "customary land rights including those held in common shall have equal force and effect in law with freehold or leasehold rights acquired through statutory allocation, registration or transaction." The challenge to the government is where to place the boundary lines to determine internal borders.

In this regard, legislators and policy-makers—as well as cartographers—would have to rely on two main sources of evidence relating to South Sudan's ethnic and administrative borders. These are the *de jure* and *de facto* borders.

De jure boundaries generally refer to borders whose existence and legality are recognized by both domestic and international law [Schultz, 2013]. In other words, *de jure* ethnic boundaries are those that were

---

6   The Map that defines ethnic borders as they stood on January 1, 1956, can be found at this link: http://www.bl.uk/onlinegallery/onlineex/maps/africa/largeimage136644.html (retrieved on August 18, 2020).

delineated by the British Colonial Government during the colonial era. These boundaries became official as of January 1, 1956, and are therefore recognized by the laws of South Sudan. For instance, both the government and the Opposition in South Sudan have—over time—created varying administrative units with reference to the 1956 borders. This is also the position taken by the African Union [Amadife and Warhola, 1993].

In creating the TBC to define and demarcate internal boundaries, the R-ARCSS clearly recognized the indispensability and binding power of *de jure* evidence for determining borders. It is for the same reason that the 1956 boundaries are the basis for determining the borders between the Republics of [north] Sudan and South Sudan.

De facto—better known as *oral*— borders refer to historical boundaries that describe the territorial limits of a given community's geographical location in relation to its neighbors. Sometimes, however, the existence of *de facto* borders may not be consistent with—or recognized by—national laws. Nevertheless, such borders are informally understood as describing the geographical limits of a given community's territory. *De facto* borders allow a community and its neighbors to conduct themselves as if these borders are recognized by law. In this regard, the determination of internal boundaries in South Sudan by the government should rely on both sources—*de facto* and *de jure* borders.

A major caveat, however, is that in the event of an inconsistency between *de jure* and *de facto* evidence, *de jure* evidence (the 1956 boundaries in this case) must supersede *de facto* evidence (the historical boundaries).

In summary, a nationwide demarcation of internal borders has the potential to mitigate ongoing border conflicts between different administrative units (states and administrative areas) as well as between communities. The government should, therefore, take the determination of internal borders very seriously because a peaceful pursuit of opportunities for sustainable livelihoods in South Sudan depends in part, on the resolution of border disputes

VII. Conclusions

Most newly independent countries face a myriad of stability challenges. In this connection, it is no surprise that the Republic of South Sudan, the world's youngest country, is confronted with monumental stability challenges. For heuristic purposes of this chapter, these challenges can be grouped into two classes.

First, South Sudan gained its independence against the backdrop of many decades of atrocious civil wars with various (northern) Sudanese dominated governments. These wars significantly undermined institutional, cultural, and political development, having almost entirely destroyed South Sudan's socio-economic and political structures. This state of affairs left the country virtually with little to no institutional and organizational infrastructure. For a country that is trying to recover its shattered soul following many decades of war and violence, these challenges are too enormous to be easily overcome.

Second, the Republic of South Sudan was birthed at a time when the concept of a government's monopoly over the tools of authority with which it asserts social and political control over the territory and people within its jurisdiction is under siege from a myriad of internal and external forces. These forces include the adverse impacts of globalization, technology (such as the negative use of social media), transnational corporate greed, and amorphous militia forces that now compete with governments to get what they want. In particular, the ubiquity of militia forces—and their ability to challenge the government's authority in South Sudan—suggest that the idea of the legitimate use of force by the government is always being contested. This makes it difficult for the government to use force—or the threat of the use of force—to exact compliance, keep law and order and, thus, impose the rule of law.

The aftermath of the civil war that broke out in December of 2013, pitting government forces against the rebels the current South Sudan's First Vice President, Riek Machar, operates to frustrate any concerted efforts to build a viable and coherent state in South Sudan. The signing of the R-ARCSS in 2018 seemingly heralds a new era—having provided an opportunity for the Republic of South Sudan to reboot itself. Through structural and institutional reforms, for instance, the R-ARCSS promises a new future for the people of the world's youngest country. It is against this background that this chapter has examined the legal foundations of sustainable livelihoods, in the context of land reforms.

But in a world structured on the basis of sovereign nations as principal players in international relations, the existence of an independent and coherently governed state is a condition precedent for an effective pursuit of sustainable livelihoods. This claim flows from the idea that the political entity we call the state is the sole competent authority that is legally endowed with institutional, economic, and political capacities to secure for its people the means and the opportunities to achieve sustainable livelihoods. International law obligates the government of nation-states to provide a conducive environment within which its people can engage in productive activities and enjoy a dignified existence. This includes adopting land policies that are conductive for the pursuit of sustainable livelihoods. Adoption of an equitable public land policy is, thus, paramount in light of the political and economic significance that land has gained in South Sudan in recent years. Only such a policy will mitigate the on-going role of land as a source of enduring conflicts both between states and ethnic communities.

It is for this reason that this chapter extensively discussed not only the question of land. It also puts forth a legal modality and strategy by which the Government should determine South Sudan's internal borders as they stood on January 1, 1956. Such a determination would go a long way to mitigate the severity of issues relating to land grabbing, intercommunal conflict, and the associated border disputes. As well, the determination of internal borders has the potential to remedy a flawed public land policy—a policy that adversely individuals' ability to access and own land, and frustrates private investment efforts.

Finally, the need for land reforms—but especially the security of land tenure—is probably the most important national undertaking South

Sudan will have had since 2005. In light of South Sudan's burgeoning population and competition over resources, failure by the government and the people of South Sudan to address the land question can only exacerbate the explosive nature of land disputes. This unwelcome result will put in peril the pursuit of sustainable livelihoods and therefore the economic future of the world's youngest country. The persistence of land grabbing, border conflicts—and the lack of a coherent public land policy—lurk behind the cycles of violence that South Sudan has had to endure since 2013.

REFERENCES

Amadife, Emmanuel, and J. W. Warhola. 1993. "Africa's Political Boundaries: Colonial Cartography, the OAU, and the Advisability of Ethno-National Adjustment," *International Journal of Politics, Culture and Society,* 6: 533-554.

Andersen, Kirsten Ewers. 2011. "Common Tenure and the Governance of Property Resources in Asia: Lesson from Experience in Selected Countries," Land Tenure Working Paper 20, online: http://www.fao.org/3/am658e/am658e00.pdf (accessed on February 7, 2020).

Ayoob, Mohammed. 2002, "International Intervention and State Sovereignty," *International Journal of Human Rights,* 6:81- 102.

Barlowe, Raleigh. 1972. *Land Resource Economics,* Englewood Cliffs: Prentice Hall.

Bromley, Daniel, 2019, *Possessive Individualism: The Crisis of Capitalism,* Oxford, OUP.

Cohen, Roberta and Francis Deng. 1998. *Masses in Flight: The global crisis of internal displacement,* Washington, DC: Brookings Institution.

Deng, David K. 2014. "Findings of Land Governance and Assessment Framework," *South Sudan Country Report* 3, online at: http://documents. worldbank.org/curated/en/756521504872888898/pdf/119635-WP-P095390-PUBLIC-7-9-2017-10-34-1-SouthSudanCountryReport.pdf (accessed on March 13, 2020).

Deng, Francis M, *et al.* 1996. *Sovereignty as Responsibility: Conflict Management in Africa,* Washington, DC: Brookings Institution.

THE LEGAL FOUNDATIONS OF SUSTAINABLE LIVELIHOODS

Department of the Interior, Bureau of Land Management, Public Land Statistics 2015. 2016. online at http://www.blm.gov/public_land_statistics/pls15/pls2015. pdf (accessed on October 29, 2019).

De Wal, Alex. 2014, "When Kleptocracy Becomes Insolvent: Brute Causes of the Civil War in South Sudan," *African Affairs,* pp. 347-69.

Dimitrovska, Milka. 2015. "The Concept of International Responsibility of State in the International Public Law System," *Journal of Liberty and International Affairs* 1: 1-15.

Donnelly, Jack. 1985. *The Concept of Human Rights,* London: St. Martin's Press.

Donnelly, Jack. 2013. *Universal Human Rights In theory and Practice,* Second Edition, Ithaca: Cornell University Press.

Duruigbo, Emeka. 2008. "Corporate Accountability and Liability for International Human Rights Abuses: Recent Changes and Recurring Challenges," *Northwestern Journal of International Human Rights,* 6:221-261.

Feder, Gershon, and David Feeny. 1991. "Land Tenure and Property Rights: Theory and Implications for Development Policy," *The World Bank Economic Rev.* 6:135-153.

Forojalla, Sibrino Barnaba and Kennedy Crispo Galla, Eds. 2010. *Land Tenure Issues in Southern Sudan: Key Findings and Recommendations for Southern Sudan Land Policy,* Juba: USAID.

Fox-Decent, Evan. 2011. *Sovereignty's Promise: The State as Fiduciary*, Oxford: Oxford University Press.

Gilroy, Paul and Joe Sim. 1985. "Law, Order and the State of the Left," *Capital and Class,* 9:15.

IGAD. 2019. *Revitalized Agreement on the Resolution of the Conflict in the Republic of South Sudan.*

Julius, Ajoe Noel. 2015. "Land Ownership and Conflict of Laws in South Sudan," Sudan Tribune online at https://landportal.org/news/2015/08/land-ownership-and-conflict-laws-south-sudan (accessed on February 11, 2020).

Kant, Immanuel. 1991. *The Metaphysics of Morals,* New York: Cambridge University Press.

London School of Hygiene and Tropical Medicine. 2018. *Estimates of Crisis Attributable Mortality in South Sudan: December 2013-April, 2018,* London: LSHTM.

Macklem, Patrick. 2015, *The Sovereignty of Human Rights,* Oxford: Oxford University Press.

MacPherson, C.B., *The Political Theory of Possessive Individualism: From Hobbes to Lock*, Oxford, OUP.

Martin, Rex. 2013. "Human Rights and Social Recognition Thesis," *Journal of Social Philosophy* 4: 1-21.

Merrill, Thomas W. 1998. "Property and the Right to Exclude," *Nebraska Law Review*, 77:729-55.

Outka, Uma, 2017, "State Lands in Modern Public Law," *Stanford Environmental Law Journal*, 36: 146-216.

Pienaar, Gerrit, 2008, "The Inclusivity of Communal Land Tenure: A Redefinition of Ownership

in Canada and South Africa," *Electronic Journal of Comparative Law,* 12: 1-5

Qadeer, Mohammad. 1985. *The Evolving Land Tenure System in Canada: Report No. 10,* Winnipeg: Institute of Urban Studies.

Rolandsen, Oystein H., *et al.* 2015. "A Year of South Sudan's Third Civil War," *International Area Studies Review* 18: 87-104.

Roncarelli v. Duplessis [1959] SCR. 121.

Schultz, Kenneth A. 2013. "What's in a Claim? *De Jure* versus *De Facto* Borders in Interstate Territorial Disputes," *Journal of Conflict Resolution,* 58:1059-1084.

Serrat, Olivier, 2008. "*Sustainable Livelihoods Approach,*" *Asian Development Bank.* 1-5.

The Sentry Report. 2019. "The Taking of South Sudan" (2019) online at: https:// cdn.thesentry.org/wp-content/uploads/2019/09/TakingOfSouthSudan-Sept2019-TheSentry.pdf (accessed on August 18, 2020).

Thompson, Janice E. 1995. "State Sovereignty in International Relations: Bridging the Gap Between Theory and Empirical Research," *International Studies Quarterly,* 39: 213–233.

CHAPTER 4

Food Security and Agricultural Development

Daniel W. Bromley

I. Agriculture in Disarray

The *substantive economy* of South Sudan is centered on agriculture. Oil is a momentary—a passing—distraction. On this evidence, the economy of South Sudan is flawed in every possible way. There is not a single aspect of the economy that warrants approval and optimism. Table 4.1 depicts a few aspects of agricultural life in South Sudan compared with 42 other countries in sub-Saharan Africa.

	South Sudan	Rest of Sub-Saharan Africa (42 countries)
Agriculture as Percent of GDP	11.7	22.0
Rural population as Share of Total	81.0	57.0
Annual Growth in Agricultural Value Added	- 6.3 %	3.4 %
Agricultural Employment (percent of total)	47.6	52.7
Percent of Female Employment Engaged in Agriculture	60.6	54.2
Percent of Male Employment Engaged in Agriculture	35.5	51.8

Table 4.1. Agriculture in South Sudan (average of 2015-2017)
Source: World Development Indicators

The first row might suggest that agriculture is a minor part of the South Sudanese economy and therefore not worth much attention. Two observations are in order. It is a minor part of GDP because it is so degraded and dysfunctional. Compounding this situation, the low share of GDP attributable to agriculture also reflects the momentary dominance of oil production. Another consideration warrants mention. Livestock production is a very extensive—low-valued—agricultural activity and so it is natural that agriculture's share of GDP would be low. In addition, a pastoral economy offers a more meaningful indicator of the relative importance of agriculture—the share of total population living in rural areas. In South Sudan, rural population, as a share of the total is 81 percent, compared with just over 57 percent across the rest of sub-Saharan Africa.

Of total employment in the country, approximately 48 percent is engaged in agriculture, compared to approximately 53 percent for the rest of the Continent. This lower percentage reflects the complete breakdown of agricultural markets and production—from security problems to the lack of credit and other necessary inputs. Markets for agricultural outputs are limited. A good share of fresh vegetables in Juba are imported from Uganda.

Notice the different gender make-up of the agricultural sector in South Sudan. The share of total female employment that is in agriculture exceeds the Continent's average, while the share of total male employment that is in agriculture is significantly lower (35.5 percent versus 51.8 percent). The absence of male employment in agriculture is a plausible result of historic—and on-going—civil conflict. Ominously, averaging over the three-year period 2015-2017, net agricultural income experienced a negative rate of growth.

With little reliable production and income data about the agricultural sector, it is necessary to turn attention to indirect measures. What is life like for the vast majority of South Sudanese living in rural areas?

II. The Perils of Rural Life

From Table 4.2 we see that virtually every South Sudanese citizen (95 percent of rural residents) must get by without basic sanitation services, that over 75 percent must practice open defecation, and that almost two-thirds are without proper drinking water services. It is apparent that on all counts, the South Sudanese suffer economic and social deprivations when compared to citizens elsewhere across the African continent.

	South Sudan	Rest of Sub-Saharan Africa *(42 countries)*
Percent Rural Population	80.9	57.5
Percent of Rural Population Practicing Open Defecation	75.4	23.2
Percent of Rural Population Without Drinking Water Services	64.3	50.7
Percent of Rural Population Without Basic Sanitation Services	95.0	75.4
Birth Rate (Per 1,000 People)	35.7	35.1
Death Rate (Per 1,000 People)	10.7	8.8
Female Life Expectancy	58.6	62.8
Male Life Expectancy	55.6	59.2
Lifetime Risk of Maternal Mortality (percent)	5.4	2.4
Maternal Mortality Rate (per 100,000 live births)	1,130.0	482.9
Under-5 Mortality Rate (per 1,000 live births)	98.6	73.8
Children Out of School (% of Primary School Age)	62.4	17.6
Female Children Out of School (% of Female Primary School Age)	67.3	19.3
Male Children Out of School (% of Male Primary School Age)	57.6	17.3

Source: World Development Indicators

Table 4.2. A Few Social Indicators (average of 2015-2017)

These indicators are central to understanding the agricultural sector in South Sudan. Compared to sub-Saharan Africa: (1) female life expectancy is 7 percent less; (2) male life expectancy is 6 percent less; (3) maternal mortality is 2.3 times greater; and (4) under-5 mortality rates are 1.3 times greater. As for schooling, Table 4.2 reveals that the percentage of children not in primary school is 3.5 times higher for South Sudan than it is for the other 42 countries. There are slight differences for girls and for boys.

The problems and difficulties captured in Tables 4.1 and 4.2 are the expected results—the symptoms—of an agricultural sector that is degraded, trapped, and hobbled by autarky. It is comprehensively dysfunctional. The livelihoods of South Sudan's vast rural population are miserable and debased.

III. The Absence of a Real Economy

In Chapter 2 it was argued that there is no *real economy* in South Sudan—it is all about oil. Unfortunately, oil is a fickle basis for any economy. There is no way that oil exports—indeed exports of any natural resources—can form the basis of a viable and sustainable economy. South Sudan's future requires that it begin, immediately, to create the necessary real economy that will deliver sustainable livelihoods—and food security.

At the end of May, 2020, the Food and Agriculture Organization (FAO) and the World Food Program (WFP) issued a report summarizing their recent Crop and Food Security Assessment Mission (CFSAM) to South Sudan. In the assessment, it was noted that:

> .... *aggregate cereal harvested area in the traditional farming sector in 2019 is estimated at about 929,600 hectares, over 5 percent above the 2018 level and almost similar to the average of the previous five years. The expansion in harvested area is due to an increase in the number of farming households (5.2 percent), following an improved security*

situation, which prompted about 417,000 displaced people to return to their places of origin in 2019. However, with 1.47 million individuals still displaced within the country and 2.22 million South Sudanese refugees still sheltering in neighbouring countries, the lingering impact of the prolonged conflict continues to affect agricultural activities and the overall harvested area in 2019 remained well below the pre-conflict level [FAO/WFP. 2020, p. 7].

- The FAO/WFP report went on to summarize the salient features of South Sudan's agricultural sector:
- Net cereal production in 2019 from the traditional sector, after deduction of post-harvest losses and seed use, is estimated at about 818,500 tonnes, 10 percent higher than 2018 and 4 percent below the average of the previous five years;
- Cereal production benefitted from the expansion of the harvested area and from abundant seasonal precipitation which boosted yields. However, in most flood-prone areas of the country, torrential rains triggered unusually widespread flooding, especially in Northern Bahr el Ghazal, Jonglei, Warrap, Unity and Upper Nile states, which resulted in significant crop losses;
- Infestation of migratory pests …[was] generally mild to moderate. Hence, less substantial losses were reported in 2019 compared to recent years;
- Cereal production increased from the previous year in Central Equatoria (39.7 percent), Eastern Equatoria (35.6 percent), Western Equatoria (30.9 percent), Western Bahr el Ghazal (29.1 percent), Unity (21 percent), Lakes (12.2 percent) states, while it remained mostly stable in Warrap State (+0.3 percent);
- Cereal production decreased in Upper Nile (-25.3 percent), Northern Bahr el Ghazal (-21.6 percent) and Jonglei (-4.9 percent) states. With a mid-2020 projected population of about 11.81 million, consuming on average of about 110 kg of cereals/capita/year, the cereal requirement in 2020 is estimated at about 1.3 million tonnes;

- Accordingly, an overall rounded deficit of about 482,500 tonnes of cereals is estimated in the traditional sector during the January-December 2020 marketing year, 7 percent below the deficit estimated for 2019, but still 22 percent above the 2015-2019 average;
- Prices of wheat, sorghum and maize, soaring since mid-2015, continued to increase in 2019, and in December they were 45, 75 and 90 percent higher, respectively than one year earlier. The high prices are due to a weak local currency, limited cereal supplies and the lingering impact of the conflict on trade and agricultural activities….large segments of the population are facing severe constraints in access to food and other basic services;
- The improved security situation benefited food trade and marketing operations in several areas of the country. However, market activity remains below the pre-conflict levels, mainly due to the macro-economic crisis severely affecting purchasing power, with high inflation reported to hamper credit operations;
- In January 2020, 45 percent of the population of South Sudan (about 5.3 million people) were in IPC phases 3 "Crisis", 4 "Emergency" and 5 "Catastrophe", a 9 percent decrease compared to January 2019 and also an improvement relative to August 2019. This is likely due to a slow accumulation of improvements in security, trading conditions and crop production;
- At subnational level, the highest prevalence of food insecurity was recorded in Jonglei (65.3 percent), Northern Bahr el Ghazal (54.7 percent) and Upper Nile (53.3 percent) states, almost unchanged from the same period of the previous year, likely as the result of the flood impacts. Floods also drove the increase in 2020 in the number of people in IPC Phase 5 to 40,000, all concentrated in Jonglei State….all other areas recorded improvements;
- The largest decline in population in IPC Phase 3 and higher from January 2019 to January 2020, were recorded in Eastern Equatoria, Unity, Western Bahr el Ghazal and Western Equatoria states;
- As expected, these proportions will increase in the lean period

in mid-2020: the proportions of population in IPC phases 3 and higher are projected to reach 55.4 percent in May-July 2020. This is a modest improvement relative to last year, but does not foresee any population in IPC Phase 5;

- Household food insecurity reached record levels in mid-2019 (77 percent of the population, with 33 percent severely food insecure), likely due to extreme rises in staple food prices. The situation improved by late 2019 to values lower than at the same time last year and similar to those registered in December 2016 and 2017. The largest improvements were recorded in Upper Nile, Unity, and Lakes states, while in Jonglei State flooding impacts led to a worsening of the situation;

- The dependency of households on markets for their staple food supply had a modest increase of about 3 percent in both lean period and post-harvest, interrupting a decreasing tendency since 2016. This is consistent with the reported improvement in trading conditions and commodity supply and it represents a positive development, since markets remain the most important source of cereals during the lean period. Food assistance remains a major component of the household food supply for Jonglei and Unity states;

- The pronounced vulnerability of the population to the high market prices led to record proportions of households with very high food expenditures during the 2019 lean period (78 percent against 74 percent in mid-2018), due to spikes in staple food prices;

- The situation improved towards end of 2019 when these proportions decreased to 58 percent (with 48 percent very high) lower than December 2018. The most extreme values of high food expenditure were recorded in Upper Nile, North Bahr el Ghazal, and Jonglei states [FAO/WFP. 2020].

The performance variability across regions, the strong deficits in particular areas, and the persistent problem of food security—including price escalation—combine to suggest that the agricultural sector is in peril.

IV. A Development Agenda for Agriculture: Overcoming Autarky

Two conditions are necessary for the agricultural sector in South Sudan to escape its present dysfunction. First, the absence of any market-related institutions must be rectified. Second, an organizational structure is required to operationalize the new institutions of an *internal* agricultural market. This will include a staffing commitment to bring at least 200 agricultural specialists into the government—such professionals comprising the foundation of a corps of educated and committed scientists and advisors to implement research, education, and outreach that will revitalize South Sudan's agriculture. These individuals must gain their appointment on the basis of sound scientific knowledge rather than as a political gift. This two-part imperative will slowly help the country overcome at least two generations of scientific and managerial neglect, agricultural asset degradation, institutional deterioration, soil exhaustion, and general dissolution of fragile rural livelihoods. Revitalizing agriculture first requires rehabilitating rural households. There are no shortcuts.

A. Institutional Rehabilitation

Institutions are the rules of engagement in a market economy. Paramount here are the rules of: (1) contracts; (2) debt and credit; (3) commercial practices; (4) bankruptcy; and (5) general market transactions across space and over time. These rules are necessary for market processes to work, and such rules therefore make an economy cohere and function. This constellation of essential rules—some of them customary and as old as memories permit, and some of them codified by courts and legislatures—are the functional and structural blueprints of an economy. Economic performance is similar to the structural integrity of a building—institutions are like blueprints, only more so. They are *more than blueprints* because they also allow for adaptation as conditions change. Institutions are akin to living organisms. They change when new circumstances indicate it is necessary to do so.

Given widespread autarky in South Sudan, it is obvious that the most important innovations for the nation's agriculture must focus on creating and enhancing market transactions across space. Low-cost trade must be facilitated between Renk, Akobo, Bor, Juba, and Malakal, as well as between Juba, Maridi, Yambio, Tambura, Wau, and Aweil. This need concerns protection against theft of goods in transit, insurance protocols for those goods if damaged in transit, control over legal and illegal check-points along transport routes, and any other uncertainties when goods are moving between sellers and buyers.

Once the problem of long-distance product and commodity markets has been addressed, the challenge of markets across space will have been rectified. The second priority concerns the necessary institutions to facilitate market exchange over time. That is the role of the credit sector. In Chapter 2 (Table 2.1) we saw that foreign direct investment in South Sudan is basically zero. It was also seen that gross capital formation in South Sudan is a mere 17 percent of what it is in the rest of sub-Saharan Africa. Finally, across the rest of sub-Saharan Africa, there are 65 borrowers from commercial banks per 1,000 adults. By way of contrast, in South Sudan there are 1.2 borrowers per 1,000 residents. This suggests that credit markets are virtually non-existent in South Sudan. In the absence of credit, agriculture is starved for liquidity—the "oxygen" of market exchange.

There are two aspects of agricultural credit that must be considered: (1) long-term capital investments; and (2) short-term production loans. Capital investments—amortized over multiple years—help farmers construct water management facilities, purchase farm implements, and construct necessary sheds and storage facilities. Production credit, on the other hand, covers a single agricultural year. Borrowed funds allow the farmer to acquire seeds, fertilizers (if available), gasoline and other necessary supplies, and keep the general enterprise going until the sale of crops or livestock generates necessary income. Such credit may also allow the farm family to survive until harvest and the arrival of new household income.

B. Organizational Creation

Four organizational innovations are necessary if South Sudan's agriculture is to be rescued from autarky and dysfunction. First, there must be an Office of Agricultural Policy Analysis (OAPA) under a Deputy Minister of Agriculture and Food Security in the Ministry of Agriculture and Food Security. The original staffing for this office should consist of ten well-trained economists and policy analysts. The primary function of this office will be to collect, assess, summarize, and make available the policy-relevant findings from existing agricultural research available globally—as well as in Africa.

Second, there should be an Office of Market Development in the Ministry of Agriculture and Food Security. Original staffing of this Office should consist of five agricultural economists whose responsibilities will include the creation of programs and projects to develop and sustain effective market channels for agricultural inputs and outputs.

Third, within the Ministry of Agriculture and Food Security there should be an Office of Agricultural Credit (OAC) to design and implement the two-track credit system—capital asset lending, and production lending. This Office should have an initial staffing contingent of three economists. Each OAC should offer two services: (1) an agricultural investment window at the agricultural bank of South Sudan; and (2) a production credit window at the agricultural bank. These two windows must be capitalized from oil revenues—the exact level of said capitalization subject to future considerations.

Fourth, there should be an Office of Agricultural Education and Training (OAET) whose purpose is to design and carry out programs and projects to enhance the performance of the agricultural sector. This Office should have a core staff in Juba numbering approximately five individuals. The major staffing component of this Office, however, must be located in 6-8 regional growth nodes throughout South Sudan. These regional offices of the OAET, called Offices of Agricultural Services (OAS), should have a professional staff of between 3-5 individuals each, depending on the nature of agriculture served. The success of these local service offices will depend on the effectiveness of the field staff in implementing meaningful programs. Services available through the local OAS offices should include a Legal Services Clinic, an Extension Education Office, and an electronic Agricultural Prices Service. The key to these OAS facilities will be to assure that there are qualified advisors to help farmers deal with problems as they arise. As part of the staffing arrangements, these local offices should employ a small contingent of local high-school students as trainees/interns to introduce local youth to the scientific and technical aspects of agriculture.

V. Implications

The common response to a dysfunctional agricultural sector in the developing world is found in the 2008 *World Development Report* from the World Bank. There we see four standard programmatic imperatives: (1) improve access to markets and establish efficient value chains; (2) enhance smallholder competitiveness and facilitate market entry; (3) improve livelihoods in subsistence farming and low-skill rural occupations; and (4) increase employment in agriculture and the rural nonfarm economy, and enhance skills [World Bank, 2007, pp. 18-19].

Notice the presumptions here that agricultural markets exist but must be made more accessible, that existing value chains must be made more efficient, that small-holders need help in becoming more competitive, that these small farmers require improved access to agricultural markets, that subsistence farmers and low-skilled rural workers require "improved livelihoods," and that there should be efforts to enhance skills in the rural nonfarm economy.

With very few exceptions, these rather standard prescriptions bear little relevance to the autarkic state of the agricultural sector in South Sudan. Agricultural markets barely exist, value chains in the food system are rare, small farmers must be established before they can worry about becoming "competitive" as implied here, and there is rarely a rural nonfarm economy to worry about.

Creating a real economy in South Sudan means starting from a base of very little.

REFERENCES

FAO. 2020. *Special Report – 2019 FAO/WFP Crop and Food Security Assessment Mission to the Republic of South Sudan.*

World Bank. 2007. *World Development Report 2008: Agriculture for Development.* Washington, DC.

CHAPTER 5

Jobs and Sustainable Livelihoods

Daniel W. Bromley

I. Employment as Social Engagement

In Chapter 2 we emphasized that regular work is essential to emotional thriving and stable communities. Engagement in work is essential to the full realization of being human. Unwilling idleness not only brings material suffering. Idleness gives rise to feelings of alienation from the on-going life of the community. Alienation is a psychological condition of estrangement between the individual and the world in which that individual must survive and flourish. A more serious aspect of unwanted idleness is that it can lead to civil conflict as young males confront a life without economic security and the possibility of family formation. A reliable predictor of social unrest is the unemployment rate among males aged 16-30.

What are the impediments for meaningful employment in South Sudan? Why has job creation failed to materialize? Given the mounting frustration with persistent political contestation, it is obvious that the most important challenge facing the people of South Sudan concerns how they might soon be able to get on with the urgent task of improving their fragile and vulnerable lives. This is a perilous time. The evident danger of post-war euphoria and hope even has a formal name—it is called a *revolution of rising expectations.*

Persistent unemployment defeats aspirations for a meaningful life. Marriage is difficult or impossible, and the hope for families becomes tenuous. Figures 5.1 and 5.2 show the nature of unemployment in South Sudan related to four neighboring countries in the region. The exceedingly high female unemployment rate in Sudan reflects general attitudes about women in the workplace. Focusing on South Sudan, it is apparent that the situation is perilous in terms of the hope for meaningful livelihoods for too many.

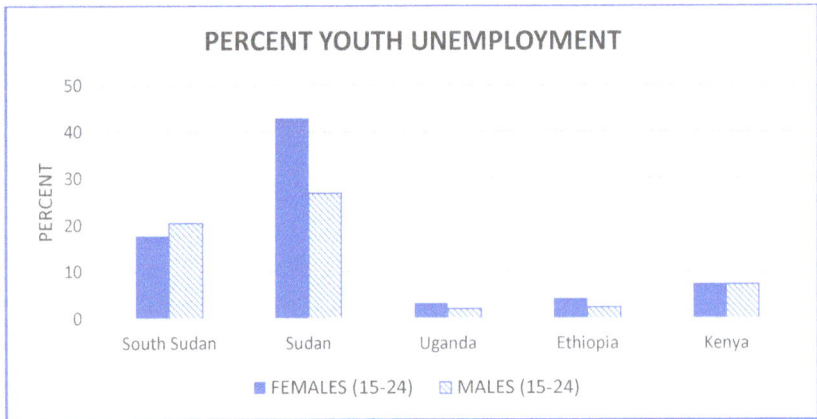

Source: World Development Indicators

Figure 5.1. Youth Unemployment Averaged over 2015-2019.

The residue of civil conflict persists. War and conflict focus the public mind on a single urgent task beyond the confines of the household. Families dedicate their labors, their every action—and even their precious children—to the existential struggle. War pulls every household into a

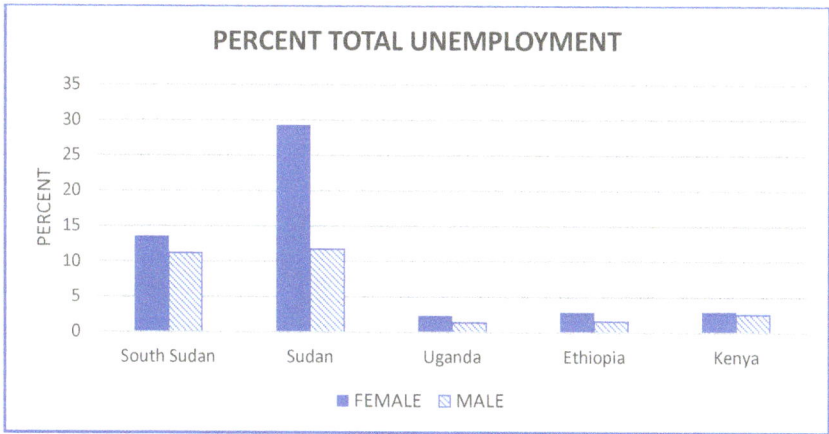

Source: World Development Indicators
Figure 5.2. Total Unemployment Averaged over 2015-2019.

particularly violent form of civic engagement in which the interests of the household become secondary. No sacrifice is too great.

Peace has the opposite effect. Once peace settles over the landscape, households once again become the center of concern and daily action. Having sacrificed so much in war, members of households now expect to reap some of the promised rewards from the emerging peace. They are willing to make similar commitments of effort and sacrifice, but the expected rewards are now different. Survival, once in doubt, is now secure.

Persistent sacrifice, effort, and struggle must soon begin to generate a gradual improvement in life's circumstances. When those improvements are scant, and when citizens notice that military conflict has been replaced by political games and power struggles, tolerance soon dissipates. Patience is exhausted.

South Sudan is faced with two profound impediments to job creation and sustainable livelihoods: (1) the economic residue of enduring civil conflict; and (2) the emergence of oil as the basis of the post-conflict economy. Unfortunately, the presence of oil compounds—indeed fuels—continued conflict. Fortunately, there is a promising future beyond oil, as we saw in Chapter 2. The world oil market is in disarray, and in the near-future the demand for South Sudan's oil will decline—if not disappear. In the meantime, however, the conjunction of persistent conflict and oil has led to the destruction of both the *structure and the functioning* of South Sudan's economy.

An economy is an evolutionary social system sustained by a variety of human interactions—some of which are monetized, and some of which are predicated on enduring personal networks. In a pastoral society this dual nature of economic interaction is of singular importance. Alliances, networks, and marriage may, to the outsider, appear as "mere" social interaction. However, every aspect of social interaction is an economic transaction in the broader sense of that term. Every social interaction is part of a household survival strategy, with both immediate and long-term implications. Decades of civil war have destroyed much of that network.

Social networks are the essence of the institutional architecture of an economy—and of a coherent state. The institutional foundations of the nation's economy and political community must now be reconstituted.

There is an additional factor in the degradation of the necessary institutional architecture for job creation and sustainable livelihoods. Specifically, there has been severe erosion in the shared cultural norm of regular employment and engagement in the world of work. Several generations of South Sudanese have now been forced to endure a life without the necessary socialization that regular wage employment offers. It is therefore necessary to re-establish the shared cultural idea of the *wage bargain*. The vast majority of young people in South Sudan have never held a regular job.

In wartime, national economies often disintegrate into isolated and compact enclaves of enforced self-sufficiency. This has certainly been the case in South Sudan. This situation is known as *autarky*. Once conflict ends, roads and bridges can be repaired, and safety ceases to be a concern. Trucks and other vehicles can gradually be shifted from military duties to commercial functions. However, overcoming autarky is a long and expensive necessity if development is to proceed. The problem is compounded by the fact that former social and economic networks have long disappeared. Moving goods across space is risky—theft is a constant threat. Necessary public services are missing. Of greater importance, autarky raises the transaction costs of re-creating traditional market relations.

Transaction costs are of three kinds: (1) the costs of learning about and then arranging possible market transactions; (2) the costs of negotiating mutually beneficial contracts—both formal and trust-based—that are the essence of market transactions; and (3) the costs of monitoring and enforcing market arrangements once they have been negotiated. The necessary institutional arrangements in an economy constitute the fundamental legal architecture whose very purpose is to reduce transaction costs.

The degraded or destroyed institutional infrastructure must be recreated as a necessary pre-condition to the reconstitution of an *internal market* across the geographic extent of South Sudan. With these institutional problems plaguing post-conflict South Sudan, inducing job creation and sustainable livelihoods will be exceedingly difficult. The problem is compounded by perverse feedbacks. In the absence of employment there is little disposable income, and with little disposable income there is insufficient demand for the output of firms. In this setting, firms have little inducement to increase employment. The population suffers from an under-consumption trap. In essence, there is little *effective demand*.

In practical terms, economic activity must be "pulled" from the autarkic hinterlands. The capital city will often be the dominant attraction in this process, but secondary places—regional growth nodes—will be essential participants in this gradual transformation.

II. Jobs and Productivity Growth

Productivity is defined as a unit of output produced by one unit of input (e.g. labor, capital). The issue of productivity growth in post-conflict societies can be difficult to address. It is obvious that labor productivity in industrial nations is high because labor-saving technology has made it possible for enormous output to be created with very few workers. Generally, labor productivity is thought of as a measure of efficiency in production. The Organization for Economic Cooperation and Development (OECD) computes labor productivity as annual Gross Domestic Product (GDP) divided by total hours worked in the same year. However, it is not easy to measure productivity unless one has detailed labor-market information such as that found in the European Labor Cost Survey Data.

But developing countries tend to have surplus labor vis-à-vis the capital stock with which that labor might be combined. This intersection between the factors of production is central to the functioning of the labor market. The standard account is that labor productivity in the agricultural sector increases because of the introduction of labor-saving technologies. As the agricultural sector evolves, and begins to rely on improved technology, newly redundant agricultural labor leaves rural areas for assorted jobs in urban areas. But of course this requires that urban jobs are increasing commensurate with the rate of out-migration from agriculture. If that does not happen, urban areas are flooded with excess labor unable to find work. This is a dangerous situation.

Over time, if this situation persists, we begin to see excess employment in the service sector. All manner of "street vendors" appear and persist. There are no jobs in urban manufacturing, and thus the under-developed formal service sector—transport, communications, tourism, education, health-care facilities—are unable to absorb excess labor. As a result, the informal "street economy" begins to expand—sidewalk barber shops, car-washing, newspaper vendors and assorted small-goods sellers choking intersections, young men "guarding" cars and jumping to clean windshields at stop lights. The informal sector brings vibrancy and danger to urban streets and intersections. These activities are clear signs of failed urban labor markets. More correctly, they are signs of the lack of suitable capital investment in the private sector sufficient to absorb redundant rural labor that has come to cities seeking employment. In the absence of formal employment, each one of these individuals has been forced to become his/her own private firm. Too often, the choices available to young women are unpleasant.

Of course the transitions under consideration in the above accounts occur (and have occurred) over several centuries in the wealthy urbanized economies now comprising the OECD. The challenge for developing countries is how, exactly, they can accomplish that long economic history in 5-10 years rather than 200 years. It is a vexing challenge that few countries have managed.

The abiding challenge in South Sudan is to develop a clear understanding about the roadmap of the transition to a sustainable growth and development path. Such a transition would normally start with emphasis being placed on job creation , even if it means—in the short-run—that the rates of labor productivity are below those prevailing in the rest of the world. The point to remember is that labor-saving technology is the enemy of job creation and social cohesion in infant economies such as South Sudan [Greenwald and Stiglitz, 2006]. In the context of South Sudan, we would expect the productivity of labor to begin to increase over time (i.e. very well into the transition path) by either: (1) increasing the use of physical capital in production so that machines, tools, and computers make each unit of labor more productive; or (2) increasing human capital such as skills training and education so that each worker can produce more per hour, day, or week.

The evidence is clear that following the Comprehensive Peace Agreement in 2005, the private sector in South Sudan—with the exception of Juba and a few other urban areas—was virtually non-existent. The government of South Sudan necessarily became the only source of non-agricultural employment. The private sector was helpless because of the complete lack of effective demand among the civilian population. Private liquidity—disposable income—did not exist. In such under-consumption traps, governments must act to stimulate effective demand. In addition, governments must also be an employer of last resort.

However, the vast majority of that early public-sector spending—pump priming—and job creation was concentrated in urban areas, despite the fact that over 80% of the population lived in rural areas. The non-salary government expenditures in urban areas have focused on constructing buildings, roads

South Sudan's Labor Force in 2008
• 72% of the population is under 30
• 50% of the population is under 18
• 83% of the population lives in rural areas
• 27% of people over 15 are literate
• 52% of urban adults, but only 22% of rural adults are literate
• 16% of adult women are literate
• 40% of adult men are literate
• Among the wealthiest 20%, 27% live primarily on wages and salaries
• Among the poorest 20%, 75% are employed in agriculture
• Among the wealthiest quintile, 30% are paid employees
Source: South Sudan National Bureau of statistics: NBHS 2009, Census 2008.

and transport infrastructure, and electric power facilities. These activities have created a demand for ancillary goods and services such as mechanics, printers, and accountants. In addition, the government has also created many urban jobs through direct employment. This prominent role for the national government over the early post-conflict period (2005-2011) drove increased spending relative to state spending. It is important to note that most public-sector jobs appear to have been created in Juba, with fewer created in the state capitals, and the smallest number created in rural areas.

The pattern of government spending was problematic. At the beginning of the Interim Period (2005-2011) there was a relatively abundant labor force—although with a very low level of human capital (only 27% of the adult population is literate). As above, the vast majority of the population (83%) lives in rural areas and depends on agriculture and animal husbandry as their primary source of livelihood. Those rural individuals are less likely to be educated, and therefore more likely to be poor. In contrast, the urban population tends to be better educated and wealthier. Those individuals and areas most in need of assistance and fiscal stimulus were the least like to receive any help.

We must recall that the initial conditions in South Sudan at the start of the Interim Period (2005) were degraded and dire. Investment in both physical and institutional infrastructures was urgently needed. The legal infrastructure (institutions) was completely lacking or inadequate. Much of that infrastructure was yet to be transformed and suitably modified from the old Sudanese legal code. The World Bank's *Doing Business* report of 2011 ranked Juba as 159th out of 183 economies. These initial institutional deficiencies are now, slowly, being addressed.

It is worth noting that recent productivity growth has been highest in those sectors where the private sector has benefited from the demand for goods and services generated by government expenditures. This is the multiplier effect at work—it is the essence of "pump priming." However, it remains true that government spending is virtually the only source of effective demand in South Sudan. After all, productivity growth is impossible in sectors with few sales.

In this regard, concerns were raised at the Consultation meeting in March, 2012 that early productivity gains were smaller in the import-competing tradable good sectors. The reason for this result seems obvious. Increased peace-time spending by the government has led to increased imports from neighboring countries, primarily because of the degraded state of those sectors in South Sudan. As the economy evolves, and as various sectors become more coherent, those imports can be expected to diminish as a share of total government spending. Indeed, that is one of the goals of creating a real economy in South Sudan to complement—and eventually supplant—the oil sector. It is imperative that import substitution activities receive special attention.

To elaborate this point, government spending during the Interim Period was concentrated in sectors producing non-tradable goods and services—construction, public administration, hotels, and restaurants. This government spending affects demand through wages paid to employees, and government procurement of goods and services. In those sectors—and areas of the country—where demand is high but supply is somewhat restricted, the private sector has responded by increasing imports, or by enhancing productivity. The relative importance of the urbanized (non-farm) private sector, especially where government spending is highest, is indicative of this trend. Figure 5.3 indicates employment across sectors from the 2008 census.

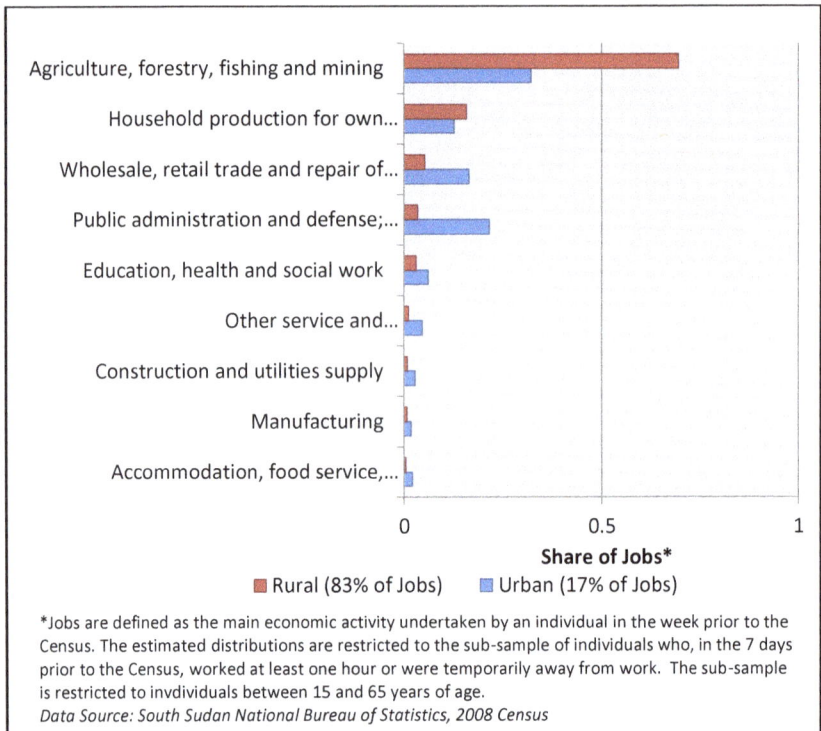

*Jobs are defined as the main economic activity undertaken by an individual in the week prior to the Census. The estimated distributions are restricted to the sub-sample of individuals who, in the 7 days prior to the Census, worked at least one hour or were temporarily away from work. The sub-sample is restricted to invdividuals between 15 and 65 years of age.
Data Source: South Sudan National Bureau of Statistics, 2008 Census

Figure 5.3. Distribution of Jobs in Rural and Urban Areas (2008)

As an example, firms in the construction sector have rapidly acquired labor-saving machines and equipment. In these non-tradable sectors, it is expected that labor productivity would increase through the import of physical capital and the training of workers. Labor productivity has also increased via: (1) importing skilled labor from abroad; (2) absorbing skilled returnees and ex-combatants into the labor force; or (3) by training the existing labor supply. The degree to which these particular productivity improvements have translated into increases in aggregate productivity depends on the size of these sectors. Unfortunately, because these sectors are relatively small, aggregate productivity gains at the national level have been rather small.

As expected, government spending priorities have been important determinants of aggregate demand, and as the private sector responds we will begin to observe selective productivity increases. As the economy evolves and matures, these productivity gains will spread throughout South Sudan. But this will take time. The export of oil, and the revenues therefrom, create a balance of payments surplus that drives down the competitiveness of import-competing sectors, and determines the relative prices of imports. Over the interim period, these factors determined the sectors in the economy that experienced the greatest increase in productivity. As above, productivity gains have been greatest in the urban non-tradable sectors. In contrast, the sector with the lowest productivity growth has been agriculture. Low government spending on non-tradable goods in urban areas has left rural areas disconnected from urban centers where demand is concentrated, and this has served to dull a major impetus for improved productivity in rural South Sudan. Government-led agricultural investment is the essential remedy to this serious problem. The agricultural potential in South Sudan, not just for domestic consumption but for export to other parts of east Africa, is profound.

This brings us to the labor supply situation in rural South Sudan. Rural areas are dominated by agriculture and assorted household production. In contrast, urban areas have begun to develop limited employment in manufacturing, construction, and accommodation services (hotels and restaurants) (Figure 5.4). It is in these sectors that we would expect the greatest productivity gains to have occurred. However, these three sectors account for less than 10% of urban jobs, which comprise only 17% of jobs in the entire economy (less than 1.7% of total jobs). Thus, productivity gains in these sectors has had a very marginal effect on aggregate productivity.

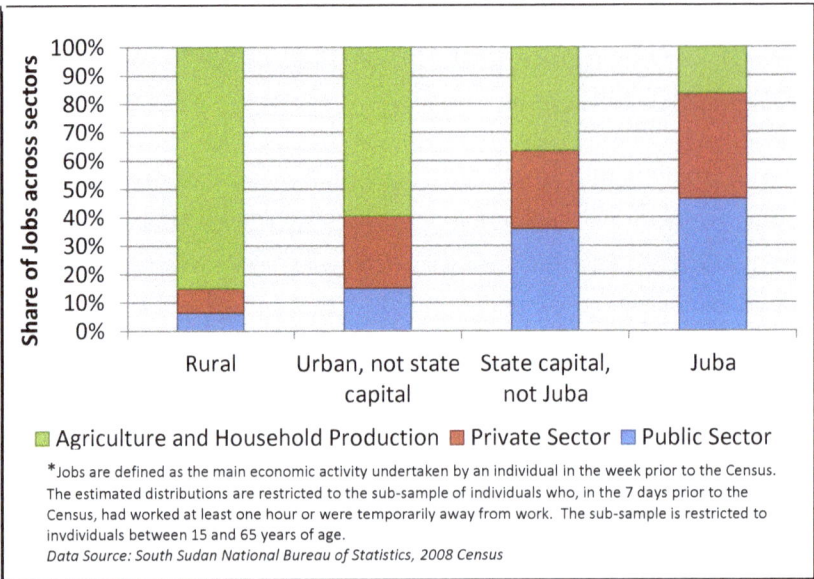

Figure 5.4. Distribution of Jobs in Rural and Selected Urban Areas.

The critical importance of agriculture as a source of jobs, as an engine of economic growth in South Sudan, is obvious. However, as above, labor productivity in agriculture has not grown at the same pace as productivity gains in urban areas. Productivity in rural areas has suffered both because demand for output is low and—despite frequent political assertions—because government spending has been predominantly focused in urban areas. Rural areas are poorly connected to markets and urban centers where demand for surplus production exists.

Although peace and stability was expected to enhance labor productivity as the return to land investment began to increase, the evidence suggests that the absence of demand in rural areas has inhibited any increases in productivity.

There is an easy explanation for this failure—agricultural producers have been forced to compete against relatively cheap imported food. Following Greenwald and Stiglitz [2006], there are often good reasons to provide protection for domestic production (and producers). This is especially the case for "infant economies," of which South Sudan is the paradigmatic case. In infant economies, still struggling to develop technology and human resources, open borders are very often harmful to the initial development of indigenous industries. This applies for agriculture as well as for manufacturing.

The current lack of demand for domestic agricultural production follows on the heels of a long period of agricultural disarray and degradation in South Sudan. We have explained this fundamental problem in Chapter 4. Beginning in the 1960s, and continuing into the present, investment in agriculture has been virtually non-existent. The shocks of two civil wars have stifled investment, encouraged defective farming methods, forced farmers to use poor seeds, and deprived them of much-needed fertilizer. Even when peace was secured, other factors have adversely affected yields. There have been long periods of drought, pests, and crop diseases, continuing internal conflicts in rural areas, as well as various trade restrictions between the two Sudans.

In the brief period between 2010 and 2011, average national net crop yields fell by 13% (from 0.75t/ha in 2010 to 0.65t/ha in 2011). Despite South Sudan's plausible comparative advantage in agriculture, only one state, Upper Nile, is engaged in mechanized farming of sorghum, sunflower, sesame and millet. Large-scale mechanized farming has the potential to enhance productivity and total output at the aggregate level [Elnagheeb and Bromley, 1992, 1994].

III. Overcoming Autarky: Regional Growth Nodes

A national capital is a natural magnet that attracts a wide variety of economic activities. The agglomeration economies of capital cities are generally too strong to resist. But nations can have only one capital city and so the existence and nurturing of secondary cities—Mumbai, Lagos, Durban, Abidjan, Alexandria, Kumasi—can be seen as an autonomous evolution of the advantages of location and economic opportunity. Those growth nodes have been slowly nurtured over the years by a variety of economic and political decisions.

The necessary first step toward recovering sustainable livelihoods is for the government of South Sudan to designate a limited number of *regional growth nodes*. These cities will then become the foundation of a regional economic development strategy. In this regard, Kapoeta, Yambio, Wau, Aweil, Rumbek, Bentiu, Bor, Malakal, and perhaps Akobo would seem to have the potential to become centers of regional economic activity. But this result will not happen without government leadership and financial support. Unfortunately, a serious barrier to the rational evolution of these growth nodes is the persistent urge to re-constitute the political landscape of South Sudan. In 2019 there was a plan to increase the number of states from the original ten to thirty-two states. The folly of this elaborate political overlay on economic potential ought to be obvious. That is, each state capital would then expect financial handouts from the central government. Rational economic structure would be sacrificed. Fortunately, that idea seems to have been abandoned.

The earlier list of regional growth nodes is tied to the likely economic activity most closely associated with each node. That is: (1) the expected importance of the activity to the country's economic future; (2) the potential impact of policy reform and targeted investments for achieving enhanced productivity and growth within the activity; (3) the extent to which the constraints to enhanced productivity and growth in the activity also seem to represent constraints that harm other economic activities; and (4) the feasibility of removing the impediments to enhanced productivity and growth through targeted investments and policy reforms.

The encouragement of regional growth nodes then opens the way to the gradual encouragement of development and population growth in and around these nodes. In essence, the institutional innovation necessary to overcome the present autarky is to create incentives for encouraging scattered villagers to become more closely linked with one of the regional growth nodes. The most obvious benefit of this regionalization policy is the opportunity to extend much-needed public services and economic opportunities to all residents. The increased concentration of population in and around the growth nodes will enhance the synergies among individuals and improve the quality of life for everyone. In addition to the creation and nurturing of regional growth nodes, several other institutional innovations—public policies—will be important ingredients in creating an integrated national economy.

A commitment to economic development in South Sudan must be cognizant of a profound employment trajectory. Economic development necessarily requires that the share of employment in agriculture will decline, while the share of employment in the various services will inevitably increase. And within the agricultural sector, the share of labor engaged in farming—agricultural production—must fall as employment in the agricultural sector shifts toward services. Included here would be agricultural research and extension, agricultural credit and marketing, technical innovation and mechanization, and veterinary services.

Outside of the agricultural sector, increased employment will gradually occur in banking, credit, insurance, law, medicine, education, real estate, and government. As an indication of future trends, services now account for 70-80 percent of total employment in the OECD countries. These trajectories are familiar throughout the world. With this inevitable transformation in employment, the essential task is to collaborate with political and economic leaders associated with the growth nodes to: (1) identify the most promising development prospects (projects and programs); (2) identify ways in which the central government can play a limited but necessary catalytic role in each of these settings and programs; and (3) secure long-term evolutionary trajectories that will produce the necessary results.

This approach allows the development of phases along each trajectory at which the central government can withdraw from its early catalytic role and turn over the enhancement and support functions to local governments, local political processes, and local economic initiative. This phased approach also allows for the gradual inducement of increased economic activity in ever-larger zones around the growth nodes. Eventual multiplier effects can then become the further stimulus for yet greater economic activity spreading out from these nodes.

IV. Program Ideas for Job Creation

The necessary institutional and organizational rehabilitation before South Sudan is able to provide meaningful livelihoods for its citizens is practically unprecedented. Not only is South Sudan not a coherent state, there *is no meaningful economy.* Even Juba, which seems to resemble a struggling capital of modest-sized African countries, is an entirely artificial construct. It is claimed that South Sudan is the world's major recipient of international assistance. The volume of traffic, and the occupancy of Juba's hotels, stand as a testament to the overwhelming international presence. If that source of income were to be removed, Juba's propped-up economy would be devastated. There is no way to deny the economic incoherence across the countryside. In this grim situation, it is necessary to search for small starts that will help to meliorate further despair. Several possibilities come to mind.

A. Youth Empowerment Scheme (YES)
There should be an immediate launch of a Youth Empowerment Scheme (YES) in the regional growth nodes. The purpose of the YES initiative is two-fold. The primary purpose is to create an activity that will teach

the discipline of structured work. But the program will also instill in the youth of South Sudan a commitment to their local community. While there is no need to design the specifics of the scheme here, several aspects seem important.

First, participation must be seen as a great honor and so there should be a limited number of spots available in each development node. Second, participation should be restricted to those youth who are entering their 7th year of schooling. In this way, there are local rewards for staying in school. The normal duration of participation should be one year so that a large number of individuals have the opportunity to participate. Third, there should be equal participation by girls and boys. Fourth, these young people should be expected to work after school, on weekends, and during the summer recess— but probably not more than 6-10 hours per week. Fifth, the YES corps of young people would be called upon to carry out any number of simple and rather routine tasks of great visibility in the local community. Collecting litter and other wastes would be one task. Keeping the school grounds and the grounds of common areas well maintained is another example. They might paint local highway markers, other signage, and carry out the pruning of trees and shrubs that block road signs or intersections. They could assist local officials in ushering and helping at public meetings.

The YES corps would be visible reminders of the importance of civic obligation. Finally, they should wear bright T-shirts in the colors of the South Sudan flag with the letters "YES" in bold colors. One important attribute of the YES initiative is that it would introduce much needed liquidity (cash) into the local economy. YES participants should receive a modest wage for their work, with the money being paid to their mother or other female adult relative. This modest payment would bestow additional esteem on the mothers (indeed the families) of the YES participants, and the incremental cash infusion would stimulate local businesses.

B. Linking Growth Nodes Through Public-Private Partnership

There is a pressing need to link the regional growth nodes with an agile truck fleet. The government could offer financial assistance to entrepreneurs who would initiate rapid transport services among the regional growth nodes. Truck owners would be required to establish prominent terminals in each of the regional growth nodes. This fleet could be an employment generator for a variety of tasks.

C. Future Professionals Program (FPP)

There is a severe shortage of well-trained staff to carry out the necessary functions of governance. A *future professionals program* would allow college students to gain experience in the public sector. The program would recruit students in their third year of college and then allow them to work part-time while completing their degree. Following graduation they would have a two-year employment contract with the national or state-level government. Skills that should be especially recruited would include accountancy, business management, finance, human resources, pre-law, to name but a few.

D. Civic Redeployment Program (CRP)

One of the pressing challenges in a post-war economy is to find plausible re-deployment opportunities for members of the military. The *civic redeployment program* would provide an exit strategy for members of the military who are prepared to locate in one of the regional growth nodes. These re-deployed soldiers would continue to receive a portion of their military pay, but would be gradually moved into other jobs. The transition period might be for a period of 3-5 years, with the level of pay from the military gradually diminishing. At the end of the transition, these re-deployed individuals would be expected to find work in the private sector or to work at public-sector jobs.

The new awareness of youth gangs in Juba (and elsewhere) serves as a stark warning that time is short. Young boys from the countryside fall under the influence of a small cadre of rogue leaders and are beginning to threaten civil peace. This threat must not be ignored. It spreads beyond the young. The presence of oil money is a harmful drug—it lulls leaders into imagining that all is well. This is a dangerous illusion. The oil dividend in South Sudan must immediately become the endowment of a comprehensive program of employment and sustainable livelihoods. In the absence of credible action and visible results, the future of South Sudan is in doubt.

E. The Entrepreneurial Incubator

Because of the absence of a meaningful private sector, at least two generations of South Sudanese youth have missed out on the normal routine of being brought into a variety of roles in the economy. That socialization into the culture of work, initiative, responsibility, diligence, accountability, and task-completion is essential for the effective performance of the economy. The minimal private sector is stifled by the absence of this essential cohort of employees, managers, owners, entrepreneurs, and business leaders. As a result, the vibrancy of the economy is impaired. Inevitably, expatriates from neighboring East African countries fill those important roles. It is necessary to create a class of future South Sudanese entrepreneurs.

The *Entrepreneurial Incubator* would require all foreign owned (and/or managed) businesses to develop a program in which South Sudanese individuals—especially women—would be brought into paid traineeships at all levels of the company. The end result would be a program to convert—over time—foreign businesses to South Sudanese ownership. Each firm's entrepreneurial incubator program would require annual re-certification by the Office of Enterprise Development.

This initiative can be modeled after a similar program in South Africa following the end of apartheid. In those programs, many white-owned firms brought young black South Africans into various positions with the purpose of creating a new entrepreneurial class. While the South African program was voluntary, the *Entrepreneurial Incubator* program in South Sudan would be obligatory of all foreign-owned and/or managed businesses.

F. Joint Ventures

A second necessary institutional innovation would be to require that all future foreign business investments incorporate one or more citizens of South Sudan as a full legal partner in the undertaking. Given the absence of investment capital in the country, this initiative cannot be made obligatory as with the entrepreneurial incubator. But foreign firms coming into South Sudan would be required to engage in joint ventures unless that can provide evidence why they should be excused. As with the entrepreneurial incubator, this program would be designed and overseen by an Office of Enterprise Development, and departments/faculties of universities in South Sudan.

This initiative can be modeled after requirements in China dating from the "opening up" to western investments in the 1980s. Most foreign investments required a joint arrangement with Chinese firms and investors.

G. Business Academy

A third institutional innovation would be a *business academy* jointly administered by the new Office of Enterprise Development and South Sudanese universities. Each year a national competition among college seniors would identify 3-5 promising new (or reconstituted) businesses conceived by contestants. Competitors would present their business plans to an expert panel and the winners would receive small grants to launch their ideas. Necessary funding for the program would come from oil revenues.

V. Sector Priorities

Four economic activities (sectors) are essential priorities for a vibrant South Sudanese economy: (1) construction; (2) energy; (3) transport; and (3) hospitality service. Each will be discussed in turn.

A. Construction

Necessary construction activities bring a focus on the usual infrastructure needs. Central here are roads, bridges, housing, drinking water, and sanitation facilities. Funding sources for these essential projects are the concern of international donors and the government of South Sudan. However, the implementation of these activities is very much a policy decision. It is clear that indigenous financial and managerial capacity is not prepared to undertake construction on the necessary scale.

Foreign contractors will be necessary to launch and carry out much of the necessary construction activities. As above, the *entrepreneurial incubator* program will provide the opportunity to bring a meaningful cohort of South Sudanese into the construction trades—especially in the mid-range of project scale involving rural schools, village water supply and sanitation, and housing.

With sustainable peace, a program of *civic redeployment* discussed above could bring trained construction engineers out of the South Sudan military for meaningful engagement in this growth sector. This initiative offers an exit strategy for a large number of soldiers who are ready for civilian life. These soldiers could continue to receive a share of their pay from the military, but would gradually become employees, managers, and perhaps owners of a variety of new construction firms throughout the country.

B. Energy

The service sector is an essential component of a nation's infrastructure. Nowhere is this more important than in the production and distribution of electricity. At the present time, electricity service in Juba is both inadequate and unreliable. For the country as a whole, over 90 percent of the population lacks access to electricity—placing it among the least electrified countries in the world. It is claimed that over 70 percent of businesses must rely on diesel-powered generators. Hydroelectric capacity is non-existent.

The defective electricity capacity problem requires a long-term investment program, but also smart strategic assessments. In this vein, it is clear that there should be a serious emphasis on solar power. Attention must be given to liberating the country from its current dependence on fossil fuels. There is a potential for solar energy in three modalities: (1) small-scale facilities suitable for new housing construction; (2) medium-scale facilities for health clinics and small office complexes; and (3) large-scale facilities for hospitals, schools, embassies, and assorted government buildings. A solar initiative offers a promising opportunity for the creation of a supportive program of research and teaching concerning solar-power engineering and management at the University of Juba. The new program should include training and capacity-building components.

C. Transport

The second important infrastructure problem in South Sudan concerns the transport sector—including logistics. The major transport corridors of Africa are clogged with slow, overloaded, second-hand, broken-down cargo trucks no longer considered useful in Western Europe. The gas mileage is abysmal, and their average speed in West Africa, where roads are quite good, is approximately 30 km per hour. On the roads of South Sudan the average speed is probably close to 20 km per hour. A trip from Juba to Aweil, approximately 700 km to the northwest, probably requires 30-35 hours. From Juba to Yambio, approximately 350 km, trips probably require 16-18 hours. Additionally, in virtually every developing country— and this is especially pronounced in Africa—there are a number of official and unofficial "check points" along the way where various payments are demanded. Delays and traffic congestion add to the problem.

Large, inefficient, and over-loaded trucks are not just normal highway hazards—they are extremely destructive of roads and bridges. During the rainy season they can become marooned and disabled in washed-out detours, and stranded along the side of the road. The enormous size and potential payload of these trucks is, in economic terms, a profound inefficiency. Most of their cargo is merely the laborious accumulation of thousands of bags and cartons of miscellaneous freight. With minimal logistical and dispatching capacity available, getting a full load for these large trucks can be difficult and time consuming. Many trucks run empty on return trips.

Serious consideration should be given to the creation of an express-truck fleet (ETF) as discussed abover. South Sudan has an opportunity to avoid the large-truck fetish of its neighbors and create an ETF consisting of small light vans—perhaps the Toyota Hiace van. There should be a government loan program to establish such a fleet. Owners-operators would be required to establish their base in one of the regional growth nodes. They must also participate in the creation and operation of a modern (computer-based) freight logistical systems. One hundred such trucks, based in the regional growth nodes, would offer a promising transport system for South Sudan. The program would create 100 new entrepreneurs who would hire local labor, bring liquidity into the growth nodes, and link the country together into a coherent integrated national economy. The express truck fleet would create the possibility for necessary *internal trade.*

Both the energy and transport sectors could benefit from an infusion of new managerial talent. The new Office of Enterprise Development in the Ministry of Finance and Planning should initiate and support an entrepreneurial incubator for both sectors, with special emphasis on bolstering service innovation, introducing technical change, and enhancing logistics. This program would help to improve sector performance while awaiting a much-need investment initiative. Importantly, managerial enhancements can reduce the need for certain expensive investments. Capital investment and managerial quality are complementary activities.

D. Hospitality Services

Foreign ownership and management of most hotels and restaurants in South Sudan offers an ideal setting for important institutional innovations. The hospitality sector is ideally suited for the *entrepreneurial incubator* and the *business academy* initiatives. Existing hotels and restaurants need to be pressed to incorporate South Sudanese citizens into positions of responsibility and ownership. The government should seek international assistance to introduce programs that will, in most settings, gradually transfer ownership and control to citizens of South Sudan.

VI. Implications

It is an unfortunate legacy of the long civil war that the private sector in South Sudan is largely owned and managed by individuals from Ethiopia, Uganda, Kenya, and Lebanon, among other places. Economic development in South Sudan will be incomplete until such time as local citizens become owners and managers of the country's private economy. The transition will serve to loosen the grip of oil on the economy, and it will give rise to a coherent entrepreneurial class of individuals that can provide both economic and political leadership into the future. Ironically, the current economic and political incoherence is good for the business community—at least in Juba—because it brings in thousands of foreign development experts who keep hotels and the few restaurants busier than they might otherwise be. It is possible that foreign owners reap special benefits from the current degraded economy.

But the status quo is not sustainable. South Sudan will not become a coherent political community—a functioning state—until its private sector is under the control of its own citizens. In that new circumstance, owners of firms will have a financial stake in the current and future well-being of society. They will become an engine of political and economic enhancement.

REFERENCES

Greenwald, Bruce and Joseph E. Stiglitz. 2006. "Helping Infant Economies Grow: Foundations of Trade Policies for Developing Countries," *American Economic Review*, 96(2):141-46.

CHAPTER 6

The Essential Delivery of Public Services

Daniel. W. Bromley

I. The Purpose of a State

States have evolved as extensions of historic collections of families and clans. The central purpose of states is to offer collective security against external threats, and to create a constellation of services that individuals are unable to finance and provide for themselves. The survival of the idea of states resides in the obvious economies of scale in the provision of these essential services. These services consist of two broad classes: (1) a constellation of necessary goods and services that facilitate sustainable livelihoods; and (2) the necessary institutional architecture that enables individuals to go about their life reasonably secure in their social and economic circumstances.

The absence of a coherent state in South Sudan is apparent by the lack of essential government services across the full geographic extent of the nation. This absence of essential government services is the reason for—it explains—the persistence of civil conflict. When individuals cannot obtain desired goods and services from their government, they are forced to organize such services themselves, or to go without. In the extreme, they become predatory on other individuals within the nation. Here lies the root of enduring civil conflict, and such conflict further undermines state creation.

Civil conflict works against state creation in two ways. First, enduring civil conflict destroys shared ideas associated with belonging to a viable functioning political entity. Civil conflict destroys lives and livelihoods. Civil conflict also destroys perceptions of who is friend and who is foe. Second, civil conflict generates patterns of individual behavior in which physical force becomes the accepted means of achieving certain outcomes. More seriously, when conflict finally ends, those who have devoted their lives to that conflict have clear expectations about improved livelihoods now that peace has emerged. Then, when daily life remains problematic, frustration emerges and if not addressed, serious political problems may soon appear. The absence of civil conflict does not always translate into a pacified and satisfied populace. Once peace arrives, wise and alert governments pay careful attention to the rather mundane concerns of households. Failure to do so is dangerous.

South Sudan cannot become a coherent state until it becomes a reasonably functional political and economic entity. The provision of a set of public services is a necessary condition for this conversion to occur. This commitment to the provision of particular services to the citizens of South Sudan is the essence of good governance. The reality of good governance is that individuals expect particular services from their government. In return, meaningful governments respond to the desires of the governed. This reciprocity can be thought of as the *citizenship exchange.*

State building is a process of creating governance across the geographic space of a nation. Specifically, state building requires the construction and maintenance of a transportation and communication infrastructure, the provision of certain public services (schools, electricity, water and sanitation, the national defense, domestic security), and a legal structure that acknowledges and enforces various property regimes, contracts, and judicial protections.

South Sudan lacks most of these—the country is at the extreme end of governance failure. Upon gaining indepen-

> ### The Mask of Citizenship
> In notional states such as South Sudan, individuals scattered across the geographic extent of the country have no legitimate claim on the services of the government. They pay nothing to the government and the government is free to ignore them as it sees fit. There is no citizenship exchange.

dence, many African nations inherited a tradition of minimal concern for the interests of individuals scattered across the geographic extent of the new national territory. This condition of indifference and neglect is particularly evident in South Sudan. Millions of individuals are not the acknowledged subjects of the governments of such notional states. They are merely there—hidden behind the *mask of citizenship*.

II. Removing the Mask

One of the residues of enduring civil conflict is that households, villages, towns, and regional trading centers have gradually been transformed into small isolated self-sufficient entities—autarkies. As these isolated collections of individuals slowly adjust to their new condition of economic irrelevance, behaviors change. Outlooks become constricted and so interaction with other similar units of governance—regional trading centers, but especially the distant capital city—whither.

Many such places become unwilling food supply depots for the war effort. As a result, local residents gradually begin to see themselves as victims of a war that is being fought on their behalf. One of the more severe effects of this civil conflict is that boys and young men from such places gradually become absorbed into the conflict. When peace arrives, few return home—either from loss in combat or purposeful relocation to the larger towns and cities encountered in their military service. Local villages suffer a profound loss of human capital. Economic recovery is imperiled and so the future of such remote places is further undermined. Without remedial action, many villages and small towns sink further into economic and political irrelevancy.

It is necessary to understand that the provision of local public goods and services by governments is only one part of state building. Obviously, individuals scattered across the distant territory of South Sudan will benefit from improved water and sanitation services, all-weather roads, health clinics, and improved schools. Such services are important indications that the national government cares about their livelihoods and well-being.

However, a more important aspect of this presence of the government is the creation of an on-going *relational contract* between scattered citizens and their government. Such goods and services are reminders that distant villagers indeed belong to something beyond the village or local town. Seeing that the government considers their well-being to be important then encourages them to understand that they have a stake in the success of the government. Mutuality emerges.

Villagers are very astute. They understand that gifts from the distant central government are never free—something is expected in return. Most often that expected "something" is political loyalty. However, there is a more durable way to turn the gift of reliable public services into a meaningful exchange. For instance, villagers could agree to tax themselves to achieve the public services they demand. Indeed, creating local initiatives in order to generate the necessary funds as their contribution to this new transaction with the central government represents something more profound. Such collective action is a catalyst for community building at the village level. Gradually the mask of citizenship will fall away. Once it is apparent that the central government cares about remote villagers, those villagers will gradually begin to care about the central government—not as a patron, but as a partner. This is the tax bargain [Moore, 2007].

The tax bargain provides a strong incentive for politicians and citizens to resolve their differences through negotiation. On the contrary, when governments derive their necessary revenues from exports such as oil and natural gas there is little need to engage citizens in the business of governance. And when citizens figure out that they are not important to the government, problems soon arise.

The tax bargain is an essential aspect of governance and hence of sustainable development. The core idea behind the tax bargain is that the government and its citizens necessarily engage in continual transactions over the provision of specific services. It is also clear that there is negotiation over how those services will be financed.

The state requires the financial means to provide goods and services such as improved roads, electricity, education, general communications networks, a judicial system, police and security, as well as the necessary institutional architecture of a coherent state. And the citizens of South Sudan require a suite of services that only the central government can provide. Similarly, the government must be concerned that the citizens of South Sudan are satisfied with the provision of goods and services. Lacking this measure of successful performance, the required tax proceeds will fall short of what is required.

With taxation falling on individuals in the form of annual assessments against income and/or wealth, there is a mutuality of interests. Improving economic conditions bring benefits to individuals and households, and those improving conditions then yield greater revenue to the government. These reciprocal incentives induce both parties to the tax bargain—the government and citizens—to support policies and specific institutions that will encourage growth.

A second incentive property of the tax bargain is that when the provision of goods and services is supported from general tax revenues— as opposed to import or export taxes—there is constant pressure on the government to improve the efficacy with which it delivers those goods and services. If citizens are paying taxes directly tied to the expected delivery of a bundle of goods and services, they are likely to be more demanding of government to make sure that it is acting in accord with those expectations.

Third, this aspect also serves to draw citizens more directly into the broader political arena to make them more involved across a wide range of issues. We see that the tax bargain is really part of the broader *citizenship exchange*. In other words, making citizens "pay" brings them more directly into the broader arena of governance and political attentiveness. The degree of government accountability will increase.

While taxation may seem counterintuitive in a poor country such as South Sudan, it is easy to show that there is an *effective demand* for improved governance. Consider Figure 6.1.

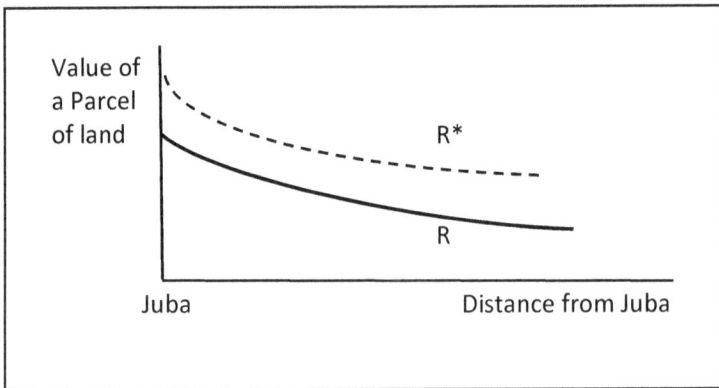

Figure 6.1. Alternative Gradients Showing Land Values

Figure 6.1 is a stylized depiction of the economic value of a parcel of land as one moves away from the capital city of Juba. The value of a parcel of land is a reflection of current (or potential) uses of that parcel. Land values in large cities are higher than land values in rural settings—this is a function of proximity to other valuable activities, as well as transport costs across distances. As one moves farther from the major city, the economic value of a parcel of land decreases.

Notice two value gradients in the Figure. The gradient R depicts the situation in a country with defective institutional architecture. South

Sudan certainly qualifies for that judgment. There are few government services, the legal environment is in doubt, transportation services are poor and insecure, and communication is difficult. There is no tax bargain—no citizenship exchange. We call such places *notional states*. In notional states, the on-going matters of life are stifled and degraded by high transaction costs. These are: (1) the costs of gaining information about promising economic opportunities; (2) the costs of arranging to engage in those opportunities; and (3) the costs of monitoring and enforcing those arrangements.

If that defective institutional architecture can be improved, the relevant land-value gradient would be shifted up (R★). This gradient reflects a constellation of institutions—legal parameters—in which there are safe and reliable transportation services, there are effective and reliable communication systems, supportive legal services are available, credit is accessible and affordable, and most markets work with reasonable efficacy. In practical terms, these new institutional arrangements—and public services—enhance the economic value of all activities throughout the nation [Nelson and Sampat, 2001]. But getting from R to R★ requires a regime of taxation and commitment on the part of both the government and the governed. The obvious reaction in a poor country will be to dismiss the possibility of such taxation. Such arguments have the reasoning precisely backwards. Taxation is the necessary condition for creating the citizenship exchange.

Notice that the *difference* between the two value gradients in Figure 6.1 is an indication of the foregone economic value driven by the present situation of defective or missing public services and associated institutions. This difference—this foregone economic value—is a measure of the *willingness to pay* of individuals for enhanced institutions and public services. This lost economic value represents the possible gains from the creation of a tax bargain. In economic terms, individuals in South Sudan have an *effective demand* for a taxation regime justified by the potential income gains that would be realized if those tax revenues were dedicated to improving the country's public services and institutional architecture.

These two value gradients show possible economic gains that would be possible if there were a coherent governance regime that facilitated the emergence of a viable economy across space. The country could thereby defeat the plague of autarky that now stalks the land.

III. But Would it Do Any Good?

In this section I make the case that investments in public services are essential to economic growth and to social well-being. The first argument to be addressed concerns the degraded condition of such services in South Sudan. In other words, we start our discussion by focusing on the urgency of great need.

The importance of investing in public services in South Sudan can be understood by consulting four data series form the World Development Indicators. Consider Figures 6.2 and 6.3. In the first figure we see a comparison of the distribution of population between rural and urban settings among five east African countries. South Sudan resembles Ethiopia in terms of the proportion of rural residences averaged over the five-year period 2015-2019. Figure 6.3 shows the rate of population growth by rural and urban residence over this same period.

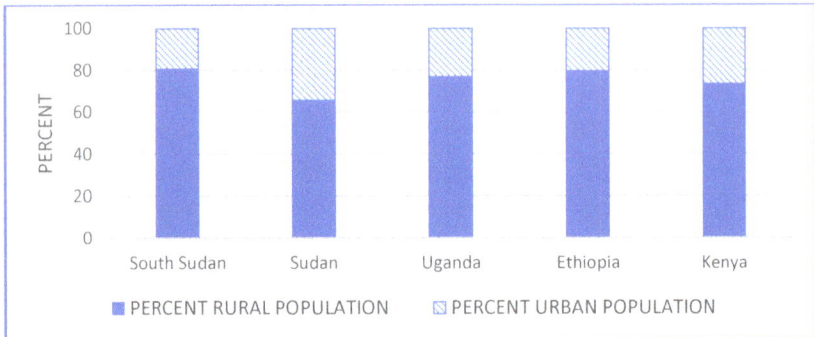

Source: World Development Indicators

Figure 6.2 Percentage of Rural and Urban Residents (averaged over 2015-2019)

The remarkable aspect of Figure 6.3 is the stark contrast with total population growth in South Sudan compared to its neighbors. Ordinarily this would be a cause for celebration. However, in this case, low population growth in both rural and urban areas is a sign of the extreme hopelessness that pervades society. The evidence from many countries is clear that when economic conditions are bad and/or deteriorating, family fertility decisions swing in the direction of reduced family size. The contrast with neighboring countries is rather pronounced.

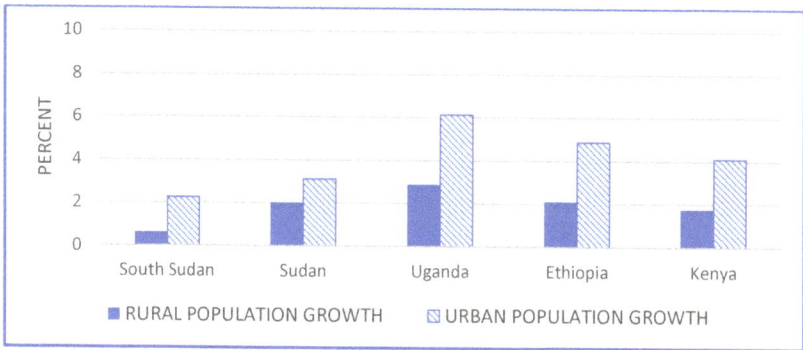

Source: World Development Indicators

Figure 6.3 Rate of Rural and Urban Population Growth (averaged over 2015-2019)

Turning now to the status of water-related public services in South Sudan, we see in Figure 6.4 that the country stands alone in the prevalence of open defecation. While it is most pronounced in rural areas, the high incidence in urban areas is more startling. Here the problem is doubly inexcusable: (1) the problem cannot be ignored by government officials who tend to inhabit urban areas; and (2) opportunities for privacy are much restricted in urban areas. Women are particularly demeaned by this necessity.

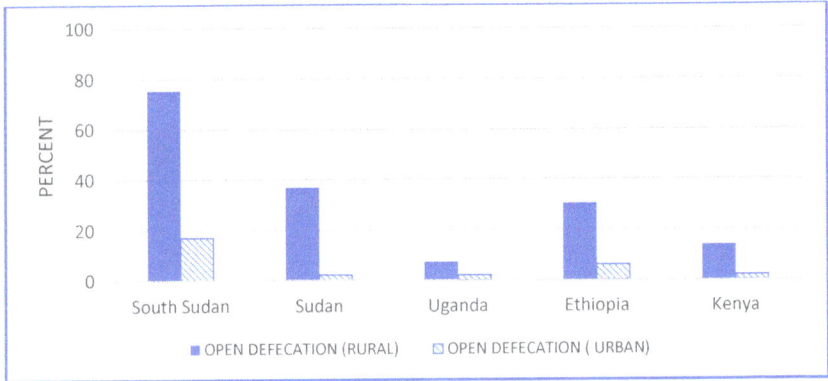

Source: World Development Indicators

Figure 6.4 Necessity for Open Defecation (averaged over 2015-2019)

In Figure 6.5 we see a variation of the data in Figure 6.4. In this second figure the focus is on the percent of the rural and urban population with access to basic sanitation services. The rural-urban disparities are very pronounced for both Sudan and South Sudan.

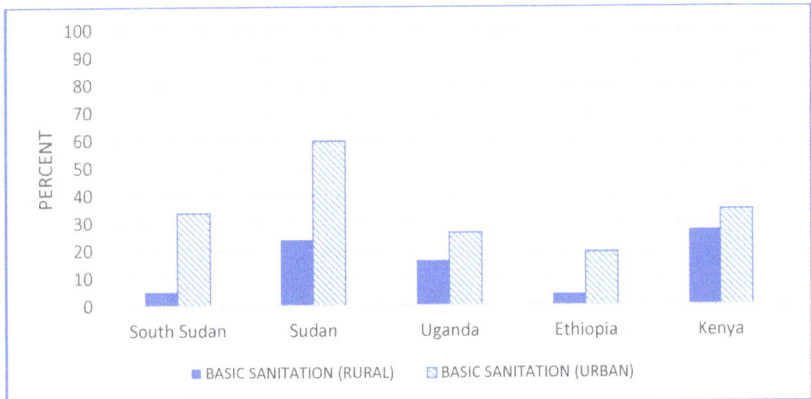

Source: World Development Indicators

Figure 6.5 Percent of Population with Access to Basic Sanitation Services (averaged over 2015-2019)

Finally we come to the problem of access to improved access to safe drinking water. Once again, rural and urban residents of South Sudan suffer in comparison with their near neighbors.

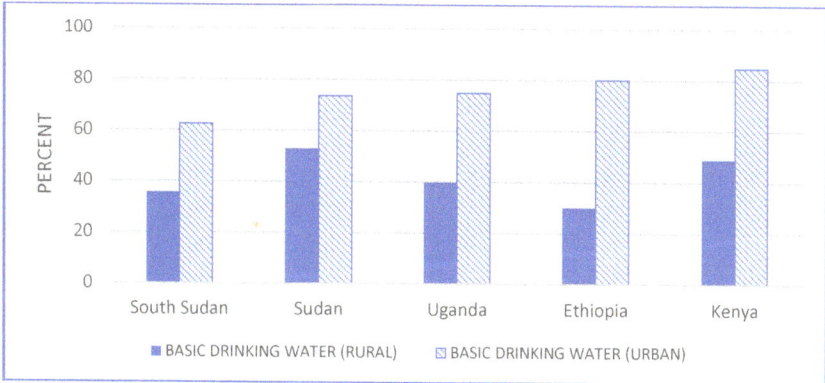

Source: World Development Indicators

Figure 6.6 Percent of Population with Access to Basic Drinking Water (averaged over 2015-2019)

The above five figures offer clear evidence that access to water-related public services is a serious problem for both rural and urban residents of South Sudan. There are two good reasons why the government should be concerned. First, access to improved water and sanitation facilities is generally considered part of the normal suite of benefits that ought to be made available to every citizen—whether they live in rural areas or in urban settings. Second, the evidence is clear that the provision of such services can make important contributions to desired economic outcomes such as household income and—therefore—a nation's GDP. This surprising role in boosting per capita incomes is worth exploring.

With that in mind, I now refer to recent analysis of over 70 countries that were—over the period 2013-2015—the poorest countries in the world [Bromley and Anderson [2018]. These countries are listed in the Appendix. The mean per capita GDP (in current US dollars), averaging across 2013-2015, was $4,046. The low figure was $577 (Central African

Republic) while the high figure was $9,723 (Namibia). Several fixed-effects econometrics models were estimated to gain an understanding of the relationship between investments in water-related public services and specific social and economic outcomes. The models presented in Tables 6.1 - 6.3 show encouraging empirical evidence that investing in water-related public services contributes to per capita GDP. They also demonstrate the multiplier effect in which several other attributes magnify the beneficial effects of providing such public services. It is no longer tenable to regard such investments as "frills" or as secondary in importance to other investments directly focused on economic growth.

Table 6.1 shows the central associations between per capita GDP and four independent (explanatory) variables in Model 1. We see four independent variables that are very highly statistically significant, with three exhibiting a positive association, and one—under-5 mortality rates—revealing a negative association with per capita GDP. It is clear that the sign of each of the variables is precisely what can be predicted from prior empirical work and economic theory.

Under-5 mortality	-0.471
Agricultural Value Added per Worker	0.347
Index of Export Value (2000 = 100)	0.149
Percent of population with rural sanitation	0.120
Observations	1,531
Number of countries	72

Table 6.1. Model 1: Highly Statistically Significant (p <0.01) Factors Associated with Per Capita GDP

The variables are to be understood as follows. A one percent *reduction* in under-5 mortality is associated with a 0.47 percent *increase* in per capita GDP. A one percent *increase* in the value added per agricultural worker is associated with a 0.347 percent *increase* in per capita GDP. A one percent *increase* in the index of export value adds a 0.149 percent *increase* to per capita GDP, and a one percent *increase* in the percent of rural residents with access to improved sanitation facilities is associated with a 0.12 percent *increase* in per capita GDP.

The interesting dimension of Model 1 is that two of the four variables shown to be positively related to increase in per capita GDP are part of a set of governance activities we would classify as "public services." These are: (1) efforts to reduce infant mortality; and (2) efforts to extend improved sanitation services to rural residents—where over 80 percent of South Sudanese live.

The suggestive variable in this first estimation—percent of rural residents with access to improved sanitation services—encourages consideration of three other water-related public services: (1) percent of the rural population with access to improved water supplies: (2) percent of the urban population with access to improved water supplies; and (3) percent of the urban population with access to improved sanitation facilities. We combined these four water-related variables into a single new variable by averaging across the four to create a variable capturing "water-related" public services. This new variable is called *access to public utilities* [Bromley and Anderson, 2018].

Table 6.2 shows the estimated results of a second model calling attention to the availability of rural and urban water-related public services across 72 poor countries. Here we see that a one percent *decrease* in under-5 mortality rates is associated with a 0.48 percent *increase* in per capita GDP. As before, agricultural value added per worker and an index of export value added both show a positive association with per capita GDP. Most importantly, we see that a one percent *increase* in the percent of the total population with access to public utilities is associated with an *increase* in per capita GDP of 0.31 percent. This is a profound endorsement of the importance of water-related public services in poor countries.[7]

---

7   Both econometric models explained over 80% of the observed variation in per capita GDP.

Under-5 mortality	-0.4808
Agricultural Value Added per Worker	0.3487
Index of Export Value (2000 = 100)	0.1476
Percent of population with access to public utilities	0.3076
Observations	1,535
Number of countries	72

The evidence seems clear from the econometric models summarized in Tables 6.1 and 6.2 that governments can bring about encouraging enhancements of per capita GDP.

The opening sections of this chapter called attention to the problematic nature of public finance in most developing countries. Specifically, there is a general absence of universal taxation—a product of poverty, the absence of a political culture of shared responsibility for shared investments (public goods and services), and weak governance that undermines trust that taxes paid will be responsibly accounted for. But the dominant reason for difficulties in such matters is the long-standing notion of political gifting. National leaders like to present themselves as the dispensers of favors and gifts. The politics of patronage is a serious barrier to creating a sense among the general population that they are responsible adults rather than dependent children whose love and loyalty can be purchased with periodic gifts. That prevailing culture dependency—of "children" who need protection and gifts dispensed by politicians—must be broken.

Of course the obvious question is how to induce individuals to submit to taxation in exchange for improved governance—consisting of a coherent suite of institutions, and a constellation of necessary public goods and services. The answer is found in *fiscal leveraging* through the establishment of *community development foundations.*

IV. Getting Started

In notional states, the only way to leverage a new regime of governance and a commitment to the provision of public goods and services is through local citizen action via means of a *community development foundation* (CDF). The purpose of a CDF is to create an arena of instrumental trust between the citizenry and the central government. This realm of trust is a necessary condition for the creation of a financial bargain between local communities who need the assistance of the central government in providing essential services that they are unable to provide on their own. Such foundations also offer a way out of the pernicious regime of political gifting that is responsible for so much corruption in the developing world.[8] The CDF brings everything out into the "daylight."

When members of a local community recognize the need for specific public services, they would first organize themselves to establish such a foundation. The next step would be to create a Foundation Board consisting of 8-10 local individuals—one-half of whom must be women. This Board would be the governing body of the foundation.

The Community Development Foundation

The purpose of community development foundations is to leverage financial resources at the village level. These financial resources then become instrumental in bringing specific public services to villages throughout the country. Villages will then be able to engage in contractual relations with the central government for the provision of desired public services.

The foundation would then create a *taxing district* as a legal body with the capacity to levy a small tax against every household in the community with the purpose of bringing specific public services to the locality. Every household in the village would be required to contribute to the foundation. I must stress that this required contribution could be exceedingly small.

---

8 The CDF is modeled after the successful Aga Khan Rural Support Programme in northern Pakistan.

The point is less concerned with raising substantial funding than it is with achieving unanimous agreement with the planned activities of the CDF and its programs. Indeed, the presence of this universal financial commitment is what development advocates often mean by the idea that a local community has "taken ownership" of a project or program. This evidence of local commitment for revenue mobilization would then enable negotiations between the foundation and the central government. One area of negotiation would be the cost-sharing protocols. The resulting contract would then serve as the terms of engagement for the planned delivery of a particular public service. Included in that contract would be a provision for cost-sharing of expected maintenance.

Notice how this differs from traditional approaches to public service provision in developing countries. The inability to mobilize revenue for local needs is invariably remedied by reliance on international donors or NGOs. Unfortunately, this merely perpetuates the politics of gifting and dependence and does nothing at all to bring local citizens into the necessary role of taking responsibility for their own enhanced community. It also fails to create meaningful linkages and constructive collaboration between citizens and their central government. Mutual alienation breeds mutual distrust. The citizenship exchange remains non-existent. The evidence is clear that business as usual simply reinforces the unwill-ingness of central governments to develop programs that can provide necessary public services to communities across the reach of the nation. State creation suffers accordingly. A vicious circle is sustained. As long as central governments are ignored and by-passed in this essential activity, they will not become partners with scattered villagers in the delivery and maintenance of public services.

V. Implications

The collaborative model recommended here can be understood as a central component of behavioral innovation. While increased access to essential public services is important, the primary purpose of this approach is to transform how central governments engage the citizenry—and how scattered villages interact with the central government. The Community Development Foundation is a central part of removing the *mask of citizenship*. This approach breaks a pervasive paralysis. Many will object to remote villagers having to tax themselves in order to receive services that the central government *ought to* provide anyway. Villagers are already poor—why should they have to offer financial inducements to central governments? Unfortunately, such thinking merely re-enforces the perverse model of the gift economy that underpins the mask of citizenship. How can we break out of this circle of blame and inactivity? The Community Development Foundation will light the way.

REFERENCES

Bromley, Daniel W. and Glen D. Anderson. 2018. "Does Water Governance Matter?" *Water Economics and Policy*, 4(3):1-32.

Moore, Mick. 2007. "How Does Taxation Affect the Quality of Governance?" *Tax Notes International*, 47(1):79-98.

Nelson, Richard R. and B. N. Sampat. 2001. "Making Sense of Economic Institutions as a Factor Shaping Economic Performance", *Journal of Economic Behavior and Organization*, 44: 31-54.

CHAPTER 7

Urgent Next Steps

Daniel W. Bromley

I. Becoming a State

The project we have undertaken here is an exercise in practical reasoning. That is, what practical steps must be taken in order that a newly independent nation can take the second essential step of actually becoming a plausible state? I opened with a reminder that a well-functioning state is a *moral community*—a group of individuals united for a common purpose, and mutually dedicated to the shared task of creating sustainable livelihoods for all. The opening thoughts of Bishop Enock Tombe Stephen remind us of the essential role of trust in human affairs. The Bishop invoked Ephesians who urged us to use our hands for good work and not for petty theft and the visitation of harm on others.

It is common knowledge that an essential obligation of a government is to protect citizens from violence at the hands of foreign malefactors. But it is equally imperative that governments protect their citizens from what is called *horizontal violence*—the visitation of harm by one group of citizens on a different group of citizens. An effective police force, and a credible justice system, must prevent such predatory behavior. Otherwise, each violent act leads to retribution which then leads to yet further violence. Soon, society is locked in a vicious circle of harm and "pay-back."

There is another dimension of unwanted predation—the oppression of individuals by their own government. This behavior is termed *vertical violence*. Well-functioning democracies protect their citizens from vertical violence at the hands of their government.

Importantly, the creation of a functioning moral community requires more than the absence of predatory behavior by governments against their citizens. The creation of a coherent and meaningful state requires that governments are an *active agent* in the creation of sustainable livelihoods. In other words, the absence of violence against citizens—either of the horizontal or vertical kind—is a *necessary* condition for a meaningful state, but it is not *sufficient*. Sufficiency can only be met when governments understand and act on their obligations to become creative agents of improved livelihoods for all who live within the boundaries of the nation.

As discussed in Chapter 1, the greatest challenge facing new countries as they emerge from civil conflict is to make the necessary transition from the logic of military combat to the logic of shared governance. Unfortunately, the governmental structure of the RTGoNU promises overlapping responsibilities, jurisdictional confusion, and—most dangerously—policy paralysis. Thirty-five ministries, scattered across five clusters, is clear evidence that this is a governmental structure motivated and justified by the need for gifted political payoffs. This is not a government built to govern. With so many political factions requiring appeasement, the R-ARCSS has built a government from the "wrong end of the stick." That is, the structure does not flow from the serious problems requiring attention—food security, meaningful livelihoods, agricultural growth, health and education. Rather, the structure has carved up governing into enclaves of opportunity for confusion.

By way of comparison, the government of Kenya consists of twenty-three ministries. Uganda comes close to South Sudan with thirty-one ministries. But Ghana has twenty-three ministries, Ethiopia has twenty-one ministries, and Sudan has twenty ministries. This is not the place to redesign the structure of South Sudan's transitional government. But it is essential to point out that the current structure of the RTGoNU represents a severe impediment to governance. The advantage of a three-year transition period is that it will expose the severe incoherence and clumsiness of this structure. The major task during the transition period will be to create a well-designed replacement.

Perhaps recognizing the structural flaws here, and in an effort to overcome the incoherencies, the R-ARCSS has embraced the idea of a *collegial presidency*. As an abstract idea this is promising. As a practical matter, it is not clear that the proposed innovation will rectify the structural flaws.

II. The Collegial Presidency[9]

Granting good intentions, the signatories to the R-ARCSS are committed to the collegial presidency as a central component of becoming a coherent and well-functioning state. This is promising. Of historical significance, all members of the collegial presidency stipulated in the R-ARCSS were central to the liberation struggle and the eventual independence of South Sudan. Now they must adopt a mental model of governance rather than one of perpetual warfare. It is also important to see the leaders of the five political groupings agreeing to share power during the transition period. That will set the proper example for the post-transition prosperity of South Sudan. This shared vision constitutes the common purpose of the collegial presidency that will provide the necessary leadership of the RTGoNU.

In that regard, the rather elaborate structural artifacts of the government of national unity, with its many officials, and its thirty-five

---

9   This discussion draws on ideas first presented in Deng, et al. [2019].

ministries, are now on trial. What must be done so that this impressive physical apparatus begins to deliver meaningful outcomes for millions of exasperated citizens who have been waiting since the euphoria of July 2011? In other words, how can the governance processes and protocols of the RTGoNU be implemented so as to induce—indeed, to require—government officials to start acting in the shared interests of the governed?

The answer to this central question—made necessary by the rather elaborate structure of the RTGoNU—is found in the concept of *governance networks*. But what do we mean by such networks? There are two kinds of networks that warrant consideration. The first is the egocentric (or dyadic) network of Figure 7.1. Here a central person interacts with a number of others in a dyadic—one-on-one—manner to accomplish tasks being orchestrated by the central figure. Hence the term "ego-centric" network. This dyadic arrangement is relevant to military campaigns, autocracies, or corporate settings where there is one central controller (boss). But the egocentric model is seriously ill-suited to coherent governance.

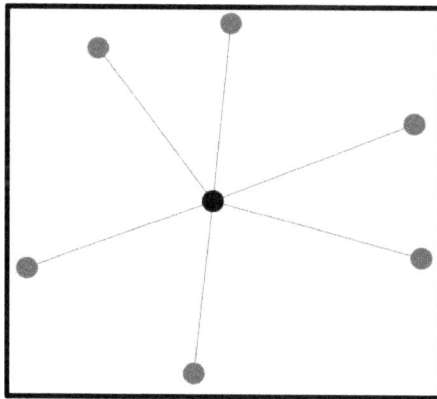

Figure 7.1 The Egocentric (Dyadic) Network

By way of contrast, coherent governance requires what is called a *whole network* model as in Figure 7.2. Notice that the whole network brings a number of other individuals—or offices—into varying degrees with each other. Some entities have dyadic ties between them, while others are linked with several others.

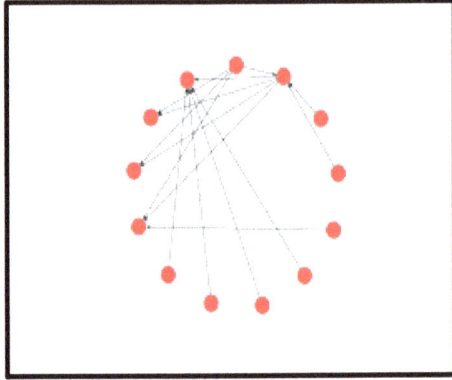

Figure 7.2 The Whole Network

As we consider the structure spelled out for the RTGoNU, there are five Vice Presidents responsible for five distinct clusters: (1) governance; (2) economics; (3) services; (4) infrastructure; and (5) gender and youth. Coherent governance in South Sudan will be impossible if each of these five Vice Presidencies falls into the trap of an egocentric dyadic model of governance shown in Figure 7.1.

Each of the five clusters will succeed in their separate mandates *only* if their constituent parts—the various Ministries—behave as shown in Figure 7.2. For instance, the Ministry of Finance and Planning, the Ministry of Petroleum, the Ministry of Mining, the Ministry of Trade and Industry, and the Ministry of Investment should have frequent and detailed engagement among themselves. At certain times, and depending on the planned activities, it will be essential for this grouping to engage the Ministry of Water Resources and Irrigation. Moreover, the Ministry of Livestock and Fisheries would necessarily be involved in certain concerns.

In other words, coherent governance will require the exquisite development of governance networks as exemplified by Figure 7.2. But more is required. If we imagine a separate *governance network* for the Infrastructure Cluster, then it is obvious that several Ministries in the Economic Cluster must be in frequent and detailed engagement with the Ministry of Energy and Dams; the Ministry of Transport; and the Ministry of Roads and Bridges.

The importance of general governance networks can be demonstrated by the even greater significance of *programmatic networks*. Very few successful government actions can be formulated, implemented, monitored, and evaluated by a specific cluster as defined in the R-ARCSS document. Such program initiatives call for the creation of special-purpose *programmatic networks*. Figure 7.3 depicts five examples of these special-purpose networks created to accomplish particular development initiatives.

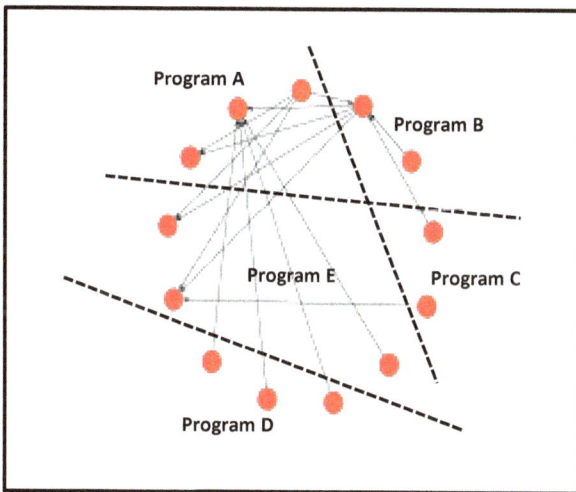

Figure 7.3 Special-Purpose Programmatic Networks

The five partitions in Figure 7.3—A, B, C, D, E—show dedicated clusters of Ministries organized around five particular development (programmatic) initiatives. These special-purpose networks must remain active and vital for specific periods of time. When the programmatic needs diminish, these particular networks can be dissolved or diminished in importance—then to be replaced by new systems networks as the need arises.

Here we see that three different Ministries are necessarily engaged in special coordinated efforts for programs A, and D. On the other hand, programs B, C, and E call for careful coordination between just two Ministries. Other examples may be imagined.

III. Implications

The collegial presidency of the R-ARCSS offers a measure of remediation for the obvious perils of a very defective structure. By carving up governance into thirty-five narrowly defined ministries, the practical business of government as an active agent for improved livelihoods has been atomized into tiny task-specific fiefdoms that almost defy logic. We will not point to specific instances, but this structure represents a dangerous example of dubious fragmentation. And then to allocate this curious governing minutia across five political factions is to invite failure.

The proposal here for *programmatic networks*—clusters—is a necessary corrective to the assured state of centrifugal chaos and paralysis inevitable in the flawed structure of the RTGoNU. With this reality almost assured, the three-year transitional period must be devoted to a serious reconsideration of this mélange of political enclaves. When the transition period is over, the government of South Sudan must be consolidated into 12-15 substantive ministries, with specialized associated functions subsumed within as sub-ministries, bureaus, offices, administrations, or departments. Only then can feasible and cost-effective governance emerge. Until that time, during the three-year transition period, we fear that we will have a great deal of government, yet very little governance. The desperate people of South Sudan deserve better.

REFERENCES

Deng, Lual A., Daniel W. Bromley, Betty A. Ogwaro, Elizabeth Pita Lugor, and Mary Ayen Majok. 2019. *South Sudan: Analytical Overview of Institutional Capacity Development Issues in The Governance and Service Delivery Clusters of RTGoNU,* Juba: Ebony Center.